In *The Gospel-Driven Church*, my friend Jared Wilson encourages us to consider the full weight of the gospel as the driver of the local church rather than metrics, which can be helpful but don't tell the whole story. By changing the driver to the gospel, we are able to change the movement from "come and see" to "go and tell." This book should soothe weary leaders' bones and free them to point passionately to the beauty of Jesus's life, death, and resurrection.

Matt Chandler, lead pastor of the Village Church,
Flower Mound, TX, president of the Acts 29 Network

Jared's understanding of church history, theology, and pastoral ministry are combined with his passion for the gospel and the local church in this helpful and insightful book. While there continues to be a desire to "change the scorecard," Jared paints a picture of what that looks like for ministry leaders. A must read for those in ministry leadership.

Eric Geiger, senior pastor of Mariners Church, Irvine, CA

The Gospel-Driven Church serves as a sobering reminder that a growing attendance does not necessarily mean a growing number of disciples of Jesus. In this book, Jared gives an honest assessment of the modern church and a solid argument for why we need to adjust our idea of how to measure a church's health. Pastors would greatly benefit from using this tool to make sure their church is moving in the right direction.

Robby Gallaty, senior pastor of Long Hollow Baptist Church,
Hendersonville, TN, and founder of Replicate Ministries

With humor, wisdom, and an easy-but-challenging writing style, Jared Wilson has offered a much-needed wake-up call to the American church. Whether you're a church planter, a pastor, or simply a Christian who desires to see your church become as healthy as possible, *The Gospel-Driven Church* serves as a road map to help shake off the shackles of "cultural relevance" and transform our churches into what God has always intended them to be.

Matt Carter, pastor of preaching at the Austin
Stone Community Church, Austin, TX

Jared Wilson contends that many churches remain unconsciously in the grip of the attractional worldview. Freedom comes by fearless inventory and swapping out the metrics by which we measure success. As one expects, Wilson is clear, winsome, and pulls no punches. Church leader, if you are looking to understand how God evaluates your hard work and whether it will produce lasting fruit, buy this book!

Dave Harvey, president of Sojourn Network, teaching pastor at Summit Church, Fort Myers, FL, founder of AmICalled.com

Jared has put into words what so many of us have felt in our guts. This book is the Magna Carta for gospel-centered change.

Clint Pressley, senior pastor of Hickory Grove
Baptist Church, Charlotte, NC

Jared's *Prodigal Church* helped us see the problem of pragmatism in the attractional church. "If it works, then work it" doesn't work anymore (if it ever did!). Multiplying noses and nickels doesn't equal faithfulness or fruitfulness. Now he offers some practical solutions to "put the gospel in the driver's seat." If you're convinced that the church needs more gospel and less gimmickry, if you want less Christian "dos" and more of Christ's "done" in your preaching, if you want the gospel to be more than a tagline at the end of message and more of an ecosystem at the center of church life, then *The Gospel-Driven Church* will help you get there.

Chris Lewis, lead pastor of Foothill Church, Glendora, CA

It's not enough to embrace the gospel. Our churches need to be shaped by the gospel. If you want to understand how to make this transition, you will love this book. I'm grateful for Jared's theological and pastoral wisdom. I wish I could have read this book twenty years ago.

Darryl Dash, pastor of Liberty Grace Church,
Toronto, Canada, author of *How to Grow*

After twenty-five years of church ministry as a gospel-loving evangelical, I found *The Gospel-Driven Church* timely, challenging, and stimulating. This book is a call to the entertainment-addicted, consumeristic church culture of the West to abandon its growth fetish and recenter on the gospel of the Lord Jesus Christ.

Steve Jeffrey, senior minister at St. Paul's Church, Sydney, Australia.

THE
GOSPEL
►DRIVEN
CHURCH

ALSO BY JARED C. WILSON

THE
GOSPEL
►DRIVEN
CHURCH

Uniting Church-Growth Dreams
with the Metrics of Grace

Jared C. Wilson

ZONDERVAN®

ZONDERVAN

The Gospel-Driven Church
Copyright © 2019 by Jared C. Wilson

ISBN 978-0-310-57787-4 (hardcover)

ISBN 978-0-310-57790-4 (audio)

ISBN 978-0-310-57788-1 (ebook)

Requests for information should be addressed to:
Zondervan, *3900 Sparks Dr. SE, Grand Rapids, Michigan 49546*

Published in association with Donald W. Gates Jr. of the Gates Group.

Cover design: Emily Weigel
Cover art: Shutterstock
Interior design: Kait Lamphere

Printed in the United States of America

19 20 21 22 23 24 25 26 27 /LSC/ 15 14 13 12 11 10 9 8 7 6 5 4 3 2

*This book is dedicated to David and Sarah McLemore,
dear friends who embody the virtues of
conviction, courage, and commitment,
and to the memory of Natalie Casco,
a dear saint who taught me much about the
power of grace in the life of the church.*

Contents

Foreword

John Henry Newman has noted how the usage of creeds throughout the history of the church has followed a predictable pattern. First, the church came together to define what it believed, identifying what was essential and excluding those who didn't embrace those essentials. Because heretics don't like to be called heretics, those who were excluded would often adjust their beliefs to fit within the parameters of the new creed while continuing to embrace many of their old heresies. As time passed, the church would need to write a new creed, using clearer (or at least different) words to further distinguish orthodoxy from heresy. With each new generation, Newman concludes, we must be prepared to rewrite our creeds to clarify the truth of God for *this* generation.

Today, phrases like *gospel-centered* and *gospel-driven* have become slogans, marks of those who hold to a new creed. Few church or denominational leaders would say they are *not* gospel-driven. But what does it mean to be *gospel-driven*?

One of the most capable pastor-theologians of our time, Jared Wilson, has undertaken the task of unpacking that phrase. Jared helps us understand what *gospel-driven* means and how we can know if our church's ministries are gospel-driven. Jared writes with wit, profundity, and clarity. He avoids the trap many proponents of the gospel-centered movement fall into—setting up a false dichotomy between depth and width. Jared explains why gospel-driven churches must, by definition, care about both.

Church leaders tend to gravitate toward either depth or width, depending on the style of their ministry or their personality. For those who go wide, success is all about the numbers—attendees, conversions, baptisms, missionaries, and weekly offerings. The numbers measure God's blessing. For those who prefer to go deep, it's about the number of Calvin's commentaries you own, how long your sermons go, how many people you expelled from the church over a disciplinary issue last year, or how well acquainted you are with 1, 2, and 3 John (John Calvin, John Piper, and John MacArthur).

Scripture doesn't leave any room for this false dichotomy. Jesus and the Apostles yearned for evangelistic width. Jesus gathered large crowds. Many people, marveling at his wisdom and authority, ran to bring their curious friends back to hear him. Jesus has more joy over one person being added to his church than anything done by the ninety-nine who are already there. When does Jesus get angry? When the religious leaders fill the Court of the Gentiles with moneychangers to assist in the buying and selling of temple animals. But his anger was not just over *what* they were doing, but *where* they were doing it. This part of the temple was for the outsider, the seeker. It was the place where all nations could come to pray. The Jews had turned this portal for the outsider into a kiosk for the insider.

Jesus did not merely come to sanctify the saved but to seek and save the lost. Jesus taught his disciples to yearn for the harvest. After Peter hauled in so many fish that his nets were breaking, Jesus said to him, "From now on you will fish for *people*" (cf. Luke 5:1–11).

Following in the steps of Jesus, the apostles also pursued explosive width. They praised God when three thousand people were saved in a single day. Evidently, they counted. They preached to as many as possible, in any secular or public arena they could find. Paul rebuked the Corinthians for not caring about the experience of the seeker in their midst, and he gave them careful instructions to make their worship services accessible and understandable to outsiders. The early church sought to spread the good news of Jesus *widely*.

But they did not pursue this width at the expense of depth. Jesus frequently preached sermons that drove out casual seekers, telling gathered crowds that unless they hated their fathers, mothers, and children in comparison to their commitment to him, they could not be his disciples. Paul spent years pouring into the same groups of believers, preaching all-night sermons to them, and writing extensive letters to instruct them more deeply in the faith. Converts in the early church were so deeply grounded in the faith that they could offer long explanations of how Jewish history pointed to Christ and could withstand even the most violent kinds of persecution (Acts 7:55–60).

A gospel-driven church cares about width *and* depth. Churches that grow deep without growing wide are probably not as deep in Jesus as they think because Jesus came to seek and save the *lost*. In the same way, churches that grow wide without growing deep are probably not as wide as they think because heaven counts disciples, not decisions. A church's ultimate impact is not only measured by the disciples it makes but in making disciples who make disciples.

The gospel is like a cyclone. The deeper you get pulled in, the farther you'll get thrust out. Charles Spurgeon—a man whose depth is well established—explained that it is possible for a fisherman to go through seasons where he doesn't catch many fish. But a real fisherman would never settle for the occasional catch: "I feel as if I lost my hope and lost my life, unless I find for my Lord some of his blood-bought ones.... I would sooner bring one sinner to Jesus Christ than unpack all the mysteries of the divine Word, for salvation is the thing we are to live for."[1]

We need to recover this gospel-spirit in our churches today, and that's what excites me about Jared's book. We don't need to put church health on the altar of numeric growth. Nor must we content ourselves with small, occasional catches of new fish. Depth in the gospel produces the boldness needed to propel the gospel message wide in an increasingly hostile culture.

I want to rejoice with Paul that in our generation the gospel is growing *deeper* in the church and wider in the world (Col 1:5–6). If that's the kind of movement you long to see in your church and in your world, read on.

J. D. Greear

Meet LifePoint Church

I t's very possible that I don't know what I'm doing."

He didn't say this aloud. It was just a whisper in his mind. But even mentally articulating this thought struck a deep chord of insecurity in Pastor Josh Cunningham. He was staring at the bookcase in his office at LifePoint Church, scanning the shelves of books, one of every four or five titles a memorial of a past season of his ministry life, like striations in a tree stump or geological sediments in a mountain. Yet as he was contemplating a vision for the future of LifePoint, he felt more like a stump than a mountain.

Josh Cunningham planted LifePoint Church twenty-two years ago with two of his best friends, Dave and Mike. The three men had met in seminary and hit it off nearly instantly. Their wives were close as well. The three couples spent a lot of time together studying, playing, and dreaming. And part of that dreaming from the very beginning was the vision for starting a church.

Josh, Dave, and Mike did everything right. They studied US demographics, researching the fastest-growing areas of the country. They drafted a prospectus and a vision document and began fundraising. Dave and Mike came from the same large church in Augusta, Georgia, and the bulk of their financial support in the first few years came from there. Besides, Mike was a natural fundraiser, so it did not take long to generate enough commitments to cover their projected expenses, including three modest full-time salaries.

The three friends had complementary gifts and callings. All three could teach fairly well, but it was decided that Josh and Dave would share most of the teaching duties, and Mike would serve as the point man for organization and administration. The three men were secure in their roles and in their relationships with each other, so there was hardly a hint of any kind of jealousy or conflict between them.

In early spring 1996, they began conducting a Sunday evening Bible study in the living room of Mike and his wife, Megan, and after a couple of months when that space was filled, a second group started meeting in the home of Dave and his wife, Darlene. And after another couple of months, when that space was filled, they began a joint Bible study in the "party room" of a steakhouse managed by one of their new attendees. Within the year, ahead of projection, they were ready to go public.

LifePoint Church launched its public worship gathering the Sunday after Labor Day, and like so many other churches launched at the time, they did so in the cafeteria of an elementary school. Josh's wife, Janet, was a talented vocalist and musician, so she led the music on her Yamaha keyboard while three church members backed her up in a simple band of guitar, bass, and conga drums.

A little over one hundred people attended their first worship service. That number dropped to sixty in the second week, and then fifty in the third. But it held steady at sixty for several months.

The product was modest at first. They were determined to stretch their budget, and since the bulk of it served to pay three full-time pastors—in retrospect, not the wisest decision for a new church not yet self-sustaining—they had to skimp on many of the "bells and whistles" they were eager to afford. The school space was relatively inexpensive, and they even had a large room on campus for storing most of their supplies and equipment, saving them money on off-site storage costs. But with Mike's shrewd financial guidance, they kept things tight and stretched every penny.

It was Easter Sunday 1997 when LifePoint really began to take off. Between regular word of mouth, strategic advertising in the surrounding community, and two mailers targeting nearby neighborhoods, they enjoyed their highest attendance yet—120.

By that time, the pastors had decided Dave should handle most of the Sunday teaching duties. Pastor Dave had an easy-going style that felt both down-to-earth and engaging. He was a creative teacher, using lots of illustrations and stories, and was quite skilled with practical application and inspiring people to a more hands-on faith. Josh was a more straightforward Bible teacher, more comfortable with verse-by-verse teaching, so he became the primary speaker at the Wednesday night gatherings LifePoint held primarily for church members and already-convinced Christians.

The Sunday morning service was unapologetically designed for seekers. The pastors had long stopped using the word *lost* to describe unbelievers, at least publicly. They didn't call them *unbelievers* either. Mike sometimes used the word *pre-Christian* because of the label's optimism, but all three had settled on *seeker*.

"After all," Pastor Mike said once in a leadership meeting, "most lost people don't think of themselves as lost. But they do think of themselves as on a quest for truth."

Thus LifePoint became one of the hundreds of churches embracing the mid-nineties model of the "seeker church." Influenced largely by Bill Hybels and Willow Creek Church in Illinois and Rick Warren and Saddleback Church in California, LifePoint wanted to see people who didn't know Jesus come to saving faith in large numbers. Can there really be a greater motivation for church than that?

Like many of their generation, Josh, Dave, and Mike felt the previous generation of church leaders had dropped the ball on this crucial mission. Yes, there had been an emphasis on evangelism and missions, but the techniques and models seemed so outdated and outmoded. Seekers didn't always follow evangelistic scripts. Seekers seemed to be asking different questions. Seekers weren't necessarily looking for a new theology or for primarily intellectual answers or even for some spiritual experience. Mostly, they seemed to be seeking a faith that made sense in their ordinary, everyday lives. The pastors were convinced that the old way of doing church wasn't working because it wasn't addressing the felt needs of lost people.

"The primary need of the seeker," Mike continued in that meeting, "is to know Jesus. But they usually feel something else first. Sometimes a sense of failure. Or just that something isn't working in their life. By addressing that need, we earn the right to speak to the deeper need. Helping people live better lives is the doorway to introducing them to Jesus."

It made great sense to everyone in the room.

"And the good news is, the Bible is so practical! It is full of application points."

The pastors came to understand that LifePoint's growth really began and gained momentum once their vision for a "church for the unchurched" started to make sense at the ground level. All the vision-casting and membership meetings explaining what they were doing certainly helped, but it wasn't until their membership, who were almost entirely previously churched couples and families, had time to see the ministry in action that something clicked, and the model made sense.

As attendance rose, so did the budget of course, and more and more money was poured into the primary mission—reaching the unchurched through dynamic, powerful, creative, and practical Sunday morning services. The band got upgraded equipment and eventually a paid worship leader (hired as the creative arts director), who began implementing more elements in the service itself, including the use of drama, video, and backdrop sets themed after Dave's different teaching series. There was more money for marketing, as well.

By spring 1999, LifePoint was regularly running 250 attendees, and by fall of that year, they began seriously shopping for a more permanent location. After a brief stint in a strip mall, which gave them more room for the worship gathering and kids' ministry but no room for pastors' offices or team meetings, they held their first service in their newly built facilities on Easter 2002. The attendance over three services amounted to 463.

"At this rate, we'll have 2,000 by 2005," Mike said. And that became his unofficial mantra. Although Dave was still the primary weekend preaching voice, supplemented occasionally by Josh, Mike was still undeniably the catalytic leader among them, the vision-caster and dreamer. He printed out the attendance goal on a banner—"2,000 by 2005"—and had it fastened to the wall in the conference room.

Most people were excited about it. It was a great goal and something tangible to work for. It was, for all intents and purposes, Life-Point's own "felt need."

And then Mike quit.

It came as a shock to most of the team, but not really to Dave and Josh, who had sensed a discontent in Mike for some time. His was an entrepreneurial spirit. He liked to start things and motivate people to join him in the movement. Once LifePoint felt up and running, the itch to do something new wouldn't go away.

Mike argued that the impact on the church would be minimal. Although Mike was fairly well-known by members, he wasn't the most public face or voice. Dave could continue teaching as always. Dave and Josh weren't so sure, but they also knew there was no way to talk Mike out of an idea once it had taken hold.

LifePoint threw a big going away party for Mike, Megan, and their kids, and Mike left to join the leadership team of a large church in Virginia.

Personally, Josh and Dave had hit a setback. It was harder than expected to replicate the leadership dynamics and organizational skills Mike brought to the table. Josh began to handle the extra administrative work that required more vision and intentionality than the routine tasks handled by their office manager. He and Dave collaborated on sermon series concepts, taking more and more cues from the worship team. The creatives began to inform the direction of the teaching emphasis more and more. Dave often had a subject he wanted to cover—family, finances, work, sex, or felt needs like confidence, peace, happiness. These were frequent topical wells he returned to time and time again, but the creative team kept the themes fresh.

Josh continued to teach on Wednesday nights and direct the small groups ministry. Since he also handled the counseling and discipleship load, his bandwidth was shrinking, so they hired an older pastor named Bob Root to serve as care pastor.

The church grew. The team grew. They didn't quite hit 2,000 in 2005, but they came close. Soon thereafter, they surpassed it.

Then Dave hit a wall.

It was 2004. He'd only been preaching eight years, but suddenly he felt like he was crumbling under the weight of the work. It was especially disorienting given how much margin the growth of the team had afforded everyone. All Dave really had to do now was prepare his weekend messages in concert with the creative team. Nobody begrudged him that. Josh knew him best and knew Dave was a hard worker who thought through every concept, expression, and line of his message over and over and over again. Dave started as a good teacher, but he had grown into an incredible communicator. The bulk of his preparation during the week involved rehearsing and memorizing his sermon so he could deliver it as naturally and flawlessly as possible, without many, if any, notes.

They wouldn't have put it this way at the time, but it wasn't the demand for Dave's productivity that had proved too much. It was the *production.*

Dave and his family returned to Augusta and spent six months with his wife's parents. Eventually he took another ministry job there.

While LifePoint had felt the impact of Mike's departure, the church entered a period of mourning upon Dave's exit. The grief was experienced at multiple levels and the recovery time was rough. Josh assumed the primary preaching role. But he taught differently than Dave. He wasn't bad—just different. More than that, Josh struggled to build the same rapport Dave had enjoyed with the creative team. People began to complain. Then they began to leave.

It was the first major crisis of Josh Cunningham's ministry life.

Fourteen years later, he faced another one.

Though it had taken almost a decade-and-a-half following the departure of Dave, LifePoint had more than recovered. Most people who attended the church now didn't even know who Pastors Mike and Dave were. Josh faithfully taught and led the church through a few life-cycles of growth. It took some time to overcome the fear of what would happen to the church after Dave's exit, but the people who remained seemed more committed to the vision than to the vision-caster, which is always a good thing. Josh stood strong, week in and week out, delivering increasingly better teaching content in an increasingly skilled way. The church experienced the kind of turnover that happened in many church-es—an almost entirely new congregation every five to seven years—and he enjoyed a well-earned reputation as a clear and compelling teacher.

With each short season of growth came shifts in emphasis. That's what led Josh to hit the books. He was always learning, always trying to grow as a leader and communicator, always trying to compensate for the gifts and skills Dave and Mike had taken with them. He went to church-growth conferences, read leadership books, listened to "best practices" podcasts, and digested practical ministry blogs.

Sometimes he wondered if this was what Dave had felt before leaving.

There was always a new idea. Always a better emphasis. Always a more innovative model. The pressure had been building for a long time, but Josh had been wise enough to offload tasks in which he was deficient to others on his team. He was an expert delegator. But he was afraid of getting left behind. One thing he'd discovered in twenty-two years of ministry was that growth didn't bring with it security. If anything, he felt more pressure pastoring a church of 2,500 than he did when it was 250. And this wasn't simply because he was the lead guy. The stakes were higher now.

Maybe he was just getting older. Maybe middle age was the problem. He increasingly felt out of the loop in creative team meetings, and each year the learning curve got steeper. He didn't catch all the pop-culture references. He felt less cool now. The fresh themes of the creatives laid over his teaching emphases didn't keep the routine from feeling stale anymore.

But it wasn't *exactly* that.

As he scanned the bookshelves and thought about the evolution of the church model they represented—one he had mirrored in his own ministry—he couldn't help but think that Mike and Dave's wall had also found him. For the first time since Dave had left, he couldn't see beyond it.

And he couldn't avoid the sinking feeling that the wall was leaning—teetering right over his head.

CHAPTER 1

The Dilemma

What if it's not working?

E very church is a church in transition.

Every church is either growing or dying. This is true even of plateaued churches, as what takes place beneath the surface of attendance numbers—the leadership process, the discipleship culture, the spirituality of the congregation—speaks more accurately to the growth or decline of a church than simply adding up how many it's "running."

In too many evangelical churches, the only transitions we see are the ones we think we're implementing.

As we come to the end of another decade of American church ministry, it's worth noting the persistent resilience of the seeker church model. We don't call it the seeker church anymore, of course. It's difficult to know what to call it. So many streams and tribes within the movement have grown in distinct ways that the seeker church of the '80s and '90s has become a veritable Baskin Robbins of church options—there are thirty-one flavors (at least) to choose from!

What began as a largely contemporary approach to church worship and corporate evangelism among some Baptists and baptistic non-denominational types has now morphed into multiple expressions with various emphases. Where Hybels and Warren were the forerunners, today's increasingly factious Christianity and the rise of more accessible media platforms has offered a plethora of experts and models, where the leading practitioner of each model becomes a distinct new brand.

The variety of styles and contexts found within this church movement gives the illusion of innovation and longevity, but when we begin
to draw comparisons, we find that they are all similar in a few central
ways—*not* theological convictions or spiritual concerns but assumptions about what best serves and attracts people. That latter concern,
attractiveness, has come to define the movement. If there is anything
that unifies the myriad flavors into a single category, it's this phrase:
the attractional church.

What Is the Attractional Church?

I (and many others) use the term attractional to refer to *a way of doing
church ministry whose primary purpose is to make Christianity appealing.*[*]

The reasoning behind the attractional church approach goes
something like this: One reason seekers aren't attracted to church
or Christianity is because they don't see the Bible as relevant to their
everyday life. Seekers ask questions and feel needs that most Christian
churches don't address. In fact, the old ways of doing church erect
unnecessary barriers between people and Jesus, barriers of religion,
tradition, judgment, and intellect. Successful ways of doing church
remove those barriers.

While the expressions are varied, by and large the attractional
church serves the end of attracting people in two ways: music and creative elements that appeal to the desired audience and teaching that is
designed to be both inspirational and practical. This is true regardless
of the size or style of an attractional church.

I also want to be clear about what I *don't* mean. When I use the
word *attractional*, I am not referring to "contemporary" worship styles

---

* Not all use the word *attractional* this way. Some apply *attractional* to a church's gracious
culture, servant-hearted posture, and apologetic thoughtfulness. Each of those things is important
for evangelism and mission. The problem is that we have perfectly good words already at our disposal
for this, words like *hospitable* and *welcoming*. What many people who commend attractional
churches are describing is a church that is attractive to outsiders because of its hold on the gospel.
Churches should be attractive in that way, but I prefer to use the word *attractional* to refer to the
church methodology that prioritizes attracting over the gospel, which repels as easily as it attracts.

or megachurches. Some critics of the attractional church movement easily lapse into a megachurch critique, and while there may be valid criticisms of megachurches, that is not my concern in this book. The size of the church isn't the point.

There are traditional and nontraditional, denominational and nondenominational, small, medium, and megasized attractional churches. Attractional is not a style. It's a paradigm.

An attractional church conducts worship and ministry according to the desires and values of potential consumers. This typically leads to the dominant ethos of pragmatism throughout the church. If a church determines its target audience prefers old-fashioned music, then that's what they feature in order to attract those people.

So while the seeker-driven megachurch is the common picture of the attractional church, plenty of smaller churches use pragmatic and consumeristic methodology in the hope of growing bigger and fulfilling their dream of becoming mega. Plenty of churches with traditional styles (music, clothing, buildings), both big and small, employ the attractional model as well. Traditional is simply "what works best" in their context.[1]

It bears mentioning that people being attracted to church is not in itself a bad thing! But when *attraction* becomes the primary mission, you tend to use whatever works to attract them. "We will do whatever it takes to get people in the door," I often hear pastors say. "We just want them to be able to hear the message of Jesus." That latter motivation is wonderful, but the problem is that "doing whatever it takes to get people in the door" can replace or undercut what we want them to be attracted to. What you win people *with* is what you win them *to*. The best motives in the world cannot sanctify unbiblical methods.

The Attractional Operating System

The attractional church is built upon two functional ideologies: *consumerism* and *pragmatism*. In considering its reach, the attractional church is essentially asking: Who is our customer? What does our customer want?

Not all those who adopt the attractional paradigm use "customer" language, but the concepts they employ are not all that different from the consumerism they reflect. Very often, what the customer wants is *not* what the customer needs.

The consumerism that dominates much of our attractional church thinking is just a subset of the larger ethos of pragmatism. Pragmatism should not be confused with practicality (for there's a lot of practical wisdom in the Bible). Pragmatism is what happens when you turn practicality into a formula. The pragmatist's mantra says, "If it works, work it." When a church leader reckons that doing whatever it takes to get people in the door is reasonable so long as they hear Jesus, he is thinking pragmatically. A ministry guru who says, "If you will employ these principles, you will have an increase in attendance," is promoting pragmatism.

In nearly every circumstance in church ministry, no matter the results, pragmatism is a sinful way of thinking, if only because it does not rely on the Holy Spirit.

Attractional assumptions and presumptions aren't new. They date back to the time of the Scriptures. Whenever God's people put their trust in kings, money, strength, or size, they were thinking pragmatically. More recently, American evangelicalism can trace the current incarnation of ministry pragmatism to the days of the Second Great Awakening and the work of Charles Finney. Finney openly believed that revivals were something any knowledgeable person could generate by utilizing the right methods. Today, the spirit of pragmatism rules the world of ministry philosophies. We see pragmatism spilling from the shelves of the "Pastoral Helps" section of the local Christian bookstore or gleaming from the screens of the large ministry conferences. Whenever rightly implemented methods are said to guarantee quantifiable results, pragmatism is at work.

In this book, I want to offer more than just another critique of American pragmatism. In the next chapter, I will argue that judging a church's health purely on visible metrics is unreliable and unbiblical. But we cannot speak of consumerism and pragmatism as just another unreliable foundation for ministry. I'm convinced that we must speak of them as fundamentally *antigospel*. What do I mean?

We must take care that our employed methods don't unwittingly undercut our desired ends. In other words, what if the ways we try to attract people to Jesus actually frustrate their ability to treasure him? Or even to see him?

If consumerism is a subset of pragmatism, then pragmatism itself is a subset of a far larger problem: *legalism*.

Again, let's be clear in clarifying the difference between pragmatism and practicality. The Bible is full of practical application. God has given us commands to obey. Neither applying the Bible nor obeying God is inherently legalistic. But when we assume certain tangible or visible results from our application and obedience, we have turned from practicality to pragmatism. We've moved from holiness to legalism.

The great irony in this is that most attractional churches pride themselves on *not* being legalistic. For some pastors, the reason for adopting an attractional approach to ministry was to reject the legalism of their upbringing. The generation that gave us the church-growth movement was, in large part, reacting to the negative fundamentalism that dominated the American church for many years. This "traditional" way of doing church was characterized by an unhealthy focus on prohibitions, which came at the expense of the gospel of grace.

The attractional church leaders rightly reject this negative understanding of how to grow in holiness, which focuses on what to avoid rather than what to do. Instead, they opted for something more positive. This is why much of attractional teaching is preoccupied with "how to" messages (which are admittedly drawn from the Bible). But the application-heavy approach of the attractional model fails to address that while the negative (prohibitive) law is powerless to change people, the positive (prescriptive) law is equally powerless. Whether you are prohibiting (negatively) or commanding (positively), the law of God cannot change a single human heart to honor God. Only the *grace* of God can do that. God's law is not bad or wrong. The law's power just works differently than the gospel's power.

Because *do* and *don't* are simply two sides to the same "law coin," by trading one for the other the attractional church simply gave legalism a makeover. The attractional approach only increases the danger of legalism, since the old kind of legalism is much easier to spot, much less attractive, and much clumsier at getting us to follow along. The new legalism is clandestine and difficult to spot. Sadly, the attractional model has fooled us into thinking it offers innovation when in reality it's just grandfather's old church of legalism with a fresh coat of paint.

As the attractional church model has aged over the past decades, it has widened the gap between its points of attraction, what lures people in, and its gospel motivations. In some churches today, you may not hear Jesus mentioned or featured prominently in a message. Worship songs aim at eliciting emotions or inspiring people with positive, encouraging thoughts rather than rehearsing the gospel or teaching biblical content. Some attractional churches are reimplementing altar calls and other invitations to respond, but these invitations can feel disconnected from the messages, creating an awkward dynamic that is similar to that of the previous generation's traditional churches. We may not sing "Just as I Am" anymore, but the methods are similar: call for responses, tally the hands raised or cards signed, and celebrate another successful service.

When the gospel is peripheral, occasional, or incidental to our mission and our preaching, we cannot trust that the gospel is truly drawing and shaping those who respond. Pragmatic methodology is legalistic because *legalism is what happens when you disconnect the Christian's "do" from Christ's "done" in the gospel.*

Even if this ministry approach instills biblical principles into the hearts and minds of people for successful living, and they somehow manage to implement them well, the best we can hope for is the development of moral unbelievers. If you win people to biblical principles but fail to win them to the biblical Christ, you will simply create religious people who lack the power to change. We create tidy unbelievers.

The Attractional Church Doesn't Work

Recently, however, the cracks in the attractional paradigm have begun to show. More and more, Christians and church leaders are seeing problems with the attractional church. To be clear, attractional churches continue to grow, and the model dominates much of the Christian publishing and church resource world. When you turn on religious television, you largely find attractional preachers. When you see an ad for a big church ministry conference, it is the attractional practitioners being promoted. When you take a church planting or leadership course in a seminary or Bible college, you will likely be taught an attractional methodology.

Why not? If it works, let's work it, right?

Some are beginning to question the prevailing wisdom of the day. And not for entirely theological reasons.

Let's start with metrics. If we look at the attractional churches' own metrics and indications, the results are mixed. We are now ten years after Willow Creek Community Church's REVEAL survey,[2] which showed that the methods Willow and its network of churches had been trusting to disciple believers into more fully devoted followers of Christ weren't exactly working as planned. Since the survey results were shared, Willow has offered several reasons and solutions to address the problem. There is a renewed focus on discipleship and spiritual practices, as well as an emphasis on personal calling and mission outside the programs of the church.

But the changes fail to address the fundamental problems. And many churches that have adopted similar methods have simply ignored the results and doubled down on their original plans.

Willow was one of the forerunners of the seeker and attractional methodology, but it is no longer as influential as it once was. Some of this is due to the variety of expressions of the attractional movement today.* Yet many churches are modeled after Willow, many more are

---

* More recently, of course, we have seen the early retirement of Willow's founding pastor,

indirectly influenced by them, and these churches have not responded to the REVEAL findings, effectively ignoring Willow's brave admission that not everything worked as planned.

If today's practitioners of the attractional model won't listen to their methodological parents, how in the world can we convince them the attractional church doesn't work?

For one, *it is becoming more difficult to think of the attractional model as generationally sustainable.* We've been tracking this trend since the days of the emerging church conversation. From Gen Y on down, generally speaking, those interested in local expressions of Christian community are less and less interested in programmatic, consumeristic approaches to spirituality.[3] This is somewhat counterintuitive, because younger generations tend to be the ones most readily embracing technology and innovation. But the issue is not the use of technology or innovating new ideas; it is the lack of authenticity they sense in an overproduced spirituality. They tend to respond negatively to pop-song covers, movie-clip illustrations, and cheeky sermon series titles.

Many have seen the evolution of event-driven, attractional programming from the youth group culture of the '70s and '80s. "Not your grandfather's church!" the promotional mailers used to say. Except now it *is* our grandfather's church. Twenty years ago Gen-X leaders attempted their own version of this, merging the attractional ethos with an older aesthetic, and the result—voila!—was the emerging church. When you couple the millennial tendency to value authenticity with a growing affection for vintage, retro, analog, organic, artisanal, what have you, the result is a cultural aversion to packaged, programmatic Christianity.

I realize this next example is anecdotal, but after writing my previous critique of the attractional church model, *The Prodigal Church,* I received many letters and emails. That book was written primarily

---

Bill Hybels, in the wake of numerous allegations of sexual immorality and harassment and the subsequent fallout within the church's leadership. These events only add to the waning influence of Willow Creek on the larger church scene.

for lead or teaching pastors in attractional churches, yet most of the responses I received came from younger pastors, most involved in student ministry or associate pastors in the "second" or "third chair." Some of them see the model as a dinosaur, just waiting for the asteroid of generational succession.

Second, *the discipleship culture of the attractional church is ecclesiologically unsustainable.* To put it another way, the undiscipled chickens are coming home to roost.

The theory goes something like this: the less gospel the attractional church offers, the less biblical conviction it has, and the less compelling it becomes to both prospective irreligious consumers *and* current religious customers. The first problem parallels trends we see in mainline churches. These are churches full of people now, but as attendees are fully "discipled" in the religion of therapeutic moralism—a Bible-lite inspirational self-help teaching—the less need they have for the church itself. In fact, a 2017 Gallup poll cites "sermons teaching Scripture" as the number one reason evangelicals give for attending church.[4] Commenting on the findings, *Christianity Today's* Kate Shellnutt writes, "People who show up on Sundays are looking for the same thing that has long anchored most services: preaching centered on the Bible."[5] Elsewhere, Ed Stetzer writes,

A while back, I sat down with Craig Groeschel, pastor of Life Church in Oklahoma. I asked him what has changed about his preaching over the years. He explained that, to preach to the unchurched, he had to start preaching deeper because even the unchurched want deeper content.

In other words, those for whom sermons were being dumbed down aren't dumb. They are interested in the truth or else they'd be out golfing.

I also had a conversation with James Emery White, author of *The Rise of the Nones*—one of the best books on engaging secular people—who told me that several things at his church (which leans more seeker-friendly) have changed over the years.

One area that has changed was the depth content of the messages. Intrigued, I asked why? He said because they are trying to reach the unchurched and these are the questions the unchurched are asking.

So, it seems that some who would be classified as "seeker-friendly" are shifting their sermon content (and in the case of Willow Creek, their ministry) from having more of a pragmatic flavor to one that is more theologically deep.[6]

Turns out you can get spiritually "lite" content just about anywhere. So why go to church for it? Inspirational pick-me-ups are a click away, Rob Bell is on *Oprah* now, and you can listen to sermons on your phone. You might as well sleep in on Sunday morning.

Let me say it this way: the attractional church has spent decades discipling its customers toward a more self-involved, individualized faith, and we should not be surprised when this self-involved individualism is fully embraced, and people stop showing up to church on the weekend.

Similarly, the rate of biblical illiteracy has increased, even among evangelicals. A 2017 Lifeway Research study, for instance, showed that less than half of professing evangelicals read the Bible every day. Only 39 percent of those who attend worship services at least once a month read the Bible every day. The Barna Group notes the gradual but significant decrease in Bible reading among Americans in general this way:

In the last six years alone, we've seen unprecedented changes. Nearly a quarter of a century ago in 1991, 45 percent of American adults told Barna they read the Bible at least once a week. In 2009, 46 percent reported doing so. These percentages were remarkably consistent over the course of nearly two decades. But since 2009, Bible reading has become less widespread, especially among the youngest adults. As more and more Millennials join the ranks of adulthood, the national average continues to weaken. Today, about one-third of all American adults report reading the Bible once a week or more. The percentage is highest among Elders (49%) and lowest among Millennials (24%).[7]

Perhaps the way the Bible has been preached and taught in the dominant form of evangelicalism over the last thirty years has something to do with this trend? When you have influential church leaders undermining the sufficiency and potency of Scripture, it will lead to fewer people reading their Bibles. Many attractional preachers use Bible verses, but this is not the same as preaching the Bible. (More on that in chapter 5.)

Today's evangelicalism faces the problem of widespread ignorance about what the Bible teaches on almost every subject of import in our cultural moment, everything from the nature of the church itself to authority and governance, from the basic understanding of the gospel to the traditional teaching on sexuality. In short, evangelicalism has inadvertently discipled people away from evangelicalism.

Thirdly, *the consumerism of the attractional church wins people not to the church but to consumerism.* The discipled chickens are finding more interesting coops! Much hand-wringing has occurred over the young adult dropout rate, at 70 percent today by some measures.[8] My goal is not to add to your anxiety, but this is a problem, especially in churches that are built on attracting people to an event or service. The typical problem in these attractional churches is that the back door is as wide open as the front. Even if the church is successful in bringing in and winning converts, these converts hit a discipleship ceiling. Some of the leaders even say to the Christians who attend: "This church is not for you."

The turnover rate in attractional churches is high, especially in the "contemporary" versions. Some estimations say that the average person attends for four to seven years before moving on.[9] As true believers mature, they grow tired of feeling spiritually plateaued in their existing attractional church and move to another church. Willow's REVEAL study told us that attractional churches did much better at satisfying churchgoers who identified as less mature in their faith, while those who'd been Christians longer felt increasingly dissatisfied. A *Christianity Today* editorial cites,

> The study shows that while Willow has been successfully meeting the spiritual needs of those who describe themselves as "exploring Christianity" or "growing in Christ," it has been less successful at doing so with those who self-report as being "close to Christ" or "Christ-centered." In fact, one-fourth of the last two groups say that they are either "stalled" in their spiritual growth and/or "dissatisfied" with the church.[10]

When your customer base is made up largely of less mature believers, it gets harder and harder to sustain forward movement.

Fourth, *the attractional church is growing culturally naïve.* Why? Because the religious market is growing increasingly post-Christian. America, like the rest of the Western world, is becoming less religious, and the number of people interested in *any* kind of Christianity is decreasing.[11] This is especially true of the attractional church's target audience: middle to upper middle class white suburbanites.[12] As cultural Christianity fades, so does the potential customer base for attractional churches. And as even more people become irreligious, the churches aimed at reaching irreligious people by appealing to their "felt needs" risk becoming more irreligious themselves. As with the liberal mainline churches, this has historically been a recipe for decline.

Sadly, it is all too likely that the attractional church will continue doing the same thing it always has—namely, assuming its neighborhoods are looking for church, *but different*; religion, *but relevant*; Christianity, *but cool*—and slowly grow further out of touch with the surrounding culture.

Fifthly, and perhaps most importantly, *the attractional church is evangelistically unsuccessful.* This may surprise you, since the entire enterprise is built on reaching unchurched people. The worship gathering is designed with sensitivity to the seeker. The entire point is that lost people come to know Jesus, right? And for a long time, many churches could claim success because their numbers grew.

In 1995 Sally Morgenthaler, an early proponent of the seeker-service approach, wrote a book called *Worship Evangelism*, summarizing how to turn your worship service into an event for seekers. Her advice led to church advertising emphasizing descriptive adjectives in referring to worship and music—words like *exciting* and *vibrant*. Twelve years after writing the book, Morgenthaler had largely come to reject her earlier assertions. She had spent the previous decade visiting the churches that had adopted her "worship as evangelism" approach and had been disillusioned by the experience. She conducted some research, and here is what she discovered:

> Were these worship-driven churches really attracting the unchurched? Most of their pastors truly believed they were. And in a few cases, they were right. The worship in their congregations was inclusive, and their people were working hard to meet the needs of the neighborhood. Yet those churches whose emphasis was dual—celebrated worship inside, lived worship outside—were the minority. In 2001, a worship-driven congregation in my area finally did a survey as to whom they were really reaching, and they were shocked. They'd thought their congregation was at least 50 percent unchurched. The real number was 3 percent.[13]

Lest you assume this case is an outlier, consider the research of Scott Thumma and Warren Bird for the Hartford Institute, profiling American megachurch attendance:

> Over two-thirds (68%) of those attending a megachurch any given week have been there five years or less compared to 40% in churches of all sizes. . . . One might logically conclude that a large percentage of the new people are also new Christians. Certainly, that is what many megachurch pastors proclaim. However,

nearly everyone, including visitors, described himself or herself as a "committed follower of Jesus Christ." We think many respondents interpreted this to mean, "do you consider yourself saved" given that barely 2% (roughly 500 people among the entire 24,900 survey respondents) said they were not a committed follower of Christ. Interestingly, of those respondents who were at these churches ten years or more, a handful (36 people or 0.1%) still described themselves as not being committed Christ-followers.

Additionally only 6% of attenders said that they had never attended services prior to coming to their current megachurch. Therefore, it is clear that the majority of megachurch attenders are not necessarily new to Christianity.[14]

Granted, this research is focused on the megachurch, and not on the attractional paradigm per se, but the claims correspond. Attractional churches of *any size* claim to exist primarily to reach the unchurched, yet the data indicates that the sampled megachurches, which have expressed attractional aims, aren't reaching many unchurched people. If the most visibly successful attractional churches aren't reaching lost people at the rate intended, what hope do smaller churches have?

The movement is still relatively new, and the research is only recently emerging. But what we are learning shows us that attractional churches aren't reaching as many lost people as they think they are and that those they reach only stay through one season of life. While we cannot draw definitive conclusions from this data, it does suggest that the pragmatic, consumeristic approach to outreach has successfully won religious consumers looking for a new experience, but it also disciples them into a Christianity that leads them to move on and try *another* new experience.

We have more churches—which is great!—but we have fewer Christians.

The increasingly undeniable fact is that pragmatism doesn't *work*. At least, it doesn't work for the things the Bible calls success.

Employing the techniques drawn from consumerism and pragmatism may gather a crowd and entertain them, but it doesn't produce fully devoted followers of Christ.

The way a church wins its people shapes its people. Consumeristic values and pragmatic methodology will win consumers and pragmatists. If they aren't won *by* the glory of Christ, they aren't won *to* the glory of Christ. In the end, the attractional paradigm doesn't go deep enough. It doesn't go deep enough to cause real heart change, and it doesn't go deep enough to grow a church in the ways that count eternally.

As Pastor Josh was beginning to realize, you cannot address a problem you won't acknowledge. This is why, on a Monday afternoon, sitting in the quiet of his office with the impending collapse of his church on his mind, Josh opened up his notebook and ripped out the page with the next day's leadership meeting agenda.

CHAPTER 2:

The Metrics That Don't Tell Us Everything

Not everything that counts can be counted

Tuesday morning. Thirty minutes until the leaders' meeting.

Josh gazed down at his open notebook. The thin margin of paper left by the page he'd torn out had a shredded edge. That's how he felt right now. Shredded. The next page was blank. He'd been thinking about what to put on that page for almost sixteen hours. Nervously he clicked the pen in his hand.

It could be a messy meeting. No, it would *definitely* be a messy meeting. He was about to drop a bomb, and he wasn't sure how it was wired. This was not his way of doing things. He'd learned efficiency from Mike, clarity from Dave, and everybody on his team had come to expect a smoothly run meeting with clearly defined objectives. Discussions and brainstorming? That was for individual teams with their own leaders. But now Josh was planning to walk into the room with a blank page, and he was nervous. And excited. Of all the innovative things LifePoint had done over two decades, rethinking it all could end up being the most innovative of all.

Fifteen minutes before the meeting. And then, he had an idea.

Could he find it in time? Surely it was around the office somewhere. He remembered seeing it a while back while organizing his office, and he'd thought to keep it. Ah yes, there it was.

A few minutes later, Josh walked into the conference room without his notebook or pen. Instead, he was holding a banner, trailing in the air behind him like a sign behind an airplane. The banner read: 2,000 by 2005. The team was all there assembled around the table. Beginning at Josh's left there was:

▶ Felix Garza—executive pastor, largely responsible for overseeing facilities, finances, staffing and personnel, and other institutional administration and organization
▶ Matt Wright—creative arts director and primary Sunday morning worship leader
▶ Drake Baker—director of student ministries
▶ Sandy Thompson—director of children's ministry
▶ Rob Hecht—pastor for growth, largely responsible for overseeing small groups, classes, and anything related to discipleship or education
▶ Bob Root—pastor of care, and besides Josh, the minister who'd been at LifePoint the longest

Josh took a few pushpins from the corkboard on the wall and fastened the banner to it.

"What's that?" Drake said.

"It's something Pastor Mike made a long time ago," Josh said.

"It was an attendance goal," said Bob.

"Yes," Josh said, adding, "but it was more than that. At least, it was more than that to me. That is, up until yesterday. I think."

Drake laughed softly, but only because he had no idea what Josh was talking about. Nobody else did either, which is why they didn't laugh. More than one of them cocked their head slightly to the side, puzzled as to what Josh meant.

Josh sat down at the head of the table and looked up at the banner. His eyes were sad, and he shook his head. "It wasn't anybody's fault," he said. "But we just got a little . . ." He looked up higher now, as if gazing through the ceiling. ". . . Confused."

Felix said, "I think we're all confused," and everybody laughed.

Josh smiled. "Well, I think it's gonna be okay. I don't know how. But I think it will. But we have a lot to talk about."

Matt shifted uneasily in his seat. He didn't like long meetings and found them stifling. This looked like it was going to be a long one. He pulled his right foot into his chair and plopped his chin down on the bald knee poking through the artfully constructed hole in his designer jeans.

Josh pointed to the banner again. "You know, back when we made this sign and hung it up in our office, we had a big dream. But it was based on things we were already doing. Basically, we wanted to get so good at what we already knew how to do that God would keep sending us more people. On one level, hoping we'd reach 2,000 people by 2005 was a really audacious goal. But on another level, it was something reasonable, even expected. Our process worked. We just needed to keep working it, getting better at it, trying harder, doing more. We didn't reach our goal back then, but we've reached it, and passed it now. The principle behind this banner has been the principle of our church ever since. It was the principle behind the launch of this church. And it's the principle we work from every week. Isn't it?"

Nobody said anything at first. But then they realized Josh was actually looking at them for a response.

Rob said, "Big attendance, you mean?"

"Yeah," Josh replied. "Big attendance."

"Well, if I can say so," Rob said, "I don't think that's what drives most of us." He looked around the room. Everybody else was still holding their tongues, but a few of them were nodding in agreement. Who among them would admit they cared *only* about numbers?

"It doesn't?" Josh pressed.

"I understand the point of the sign and the point of wanting to reach more people, but I think most of us really just want people to grow in their faith."

Josh smiled. "Well, of course the discipleship guy would say that!"

Rob smiled too. "Well, yeah."

"But let's be ruthlessly honest. I know big numbers isn't what drives most of you. Or maybe any of you. I know that. But can you really deny that this idea isn't the banner flying over our church? Let me put it this way: Is the way you do ministry impacted by pressure to get more people?"

Felix spoke up. "I don't know if I can say that about my area of responsibility in the church, since mostly I'm occupied with figuring out how to lead the numbers we already have and how to make sure we don't overextend ourselves. But I would say it's not really a bad thing to want to reach more people, to want people to know Jesus."

Josh seemed chastened by this somewhat. "Yes. You're right. I just . . ." He trailed off.

Everybody looked at each other, confused. *What do we say?*

Was Josh cracking up? They'd never been in a meeting with him that started this way. Or ended this way. Or had a middle that went this way. Was this a test? What exactly was happening?

Bob, in his fatherly way, finally broke the silence. "Josh, why don't you just tell us what is bothering you and then we can figure out how to help?"

Josh loved Bob. In all their time together, he never felt unpastored by his older friend. But when Bob said, "We can figure out how to help," Josh knew he meant "We can figure out how to make you feel better." The problem was, Josh didn't think that was an option, at least for now.

"Here's what I'm thinking," Josh said, looking again at Mike's goalpost banner. "In the twenty-two years since we planted LifePoint, I'm not sure we've ever had our eyes on the right prize."

Matt's eyebrows arched over his pointy knee. Sandy chewed her lip. The others frowned. All of them, that is, except Rob, the pastor for growth, and Drake, the youth pastor. Rob and Drake leaned in.

Not All That Counts Can Be Counted

In books and blogs over the past decade, there have been ongoing discussions among church leaders contrasting *faithfulness* and *fruitfulness*. This is a direct extension of the tension every leader faces between faithfulness and success. When certain prominent teachers and writers say that success can be guaranteed by adopting a certain model or following a set of steps, it calls into question the competency of those who struggle to see similar success in their own practice. More and more, pastors frustrated with the pragmatism of the "success" camp have lauded faithfulness as the true measure of success, not results.

But doesn't the Bible promise success? Of a kind, anyway?

Enter a new generation of teachers and writers who feel the angst about success and seek to reframe it in a more biblical way—thus *fruitfulness*.

Faithfulness has become shorthand for commitment to a biblical model or ministry philosophy, regardless of attendance metrics or other visible results. Fruitfulness, on the other hand, has also been promoted as a biblical model, one that emphasizes the need for results—whether that is defined as spiritual growth, numerical attendance, giving trends, or some other metric.

In the beginning, these conversations revolved around the question of how to measure faithfulness and if it could truly be defined as success. Many leaders, of course, agree that faithfulness and fruitfulness cannot easily be pitted against each other. But the way the qualities were measured was open to debate and discussion. For instance, the faithfulness crowd seem to imply that the essential task of ministry is to work hard and do what is expected and that growing the church should not be a driving factor that motivates our ministry. The faithful crowd suspects the fruitful crowd of pragmatism.

On the other hand, the fruitful crowd seems to imply that ministers who are not concerned about the growth of their churches are not as faithful as they claim to be. They suspect the faithful crowd of . . . well, laziness, I suppose. Or simply not being good at their jobs.

Though many in the conversation have reached a truce, the success crowd appeared to compromise by acknowledging that ministers are not called to *ensure* success. But then, when pressed to define what fruitfulness looks like, many simply resorted to the metrics used to typically define success—growing attendance and giving.

We need to be careful that we're not just rearranging words.

So how do we define church growth biblically? We must hold these two principles in tension, since they each affirm a biblical truth. A ministry's faithfulness to the mission of God *is itself* success, regardless of the results. Yet at the same time, a faithful ministry *will be* a fruitful ministry. We need to take care that we define fruitful according to the biblical portraits of fruitfulness.

Does the first point mean we shouldn't care about results? No. It means we should look *differently* for results, using different standards for measuring success than the consumeristic models. Measuring a church's fruitfulness is not as simple as counting the hands raised during an invitation or tracking how many parking spots are filled.

We are at an advantage at this point in history. Not only do we have the Bible to rely on, but we also have plenty of records narrating past movements of God that can help us in developing reliable measurements of church health. In 1741 American pastor Jonathan Edwards first published his now-classic book *The Distinguishing Marks of a Work of the Spirit of God*. In this important work, Edwards analyzes and synthesizes all he's experienced in the revivals of his day (chronicled most notably in *A Narrative of Surprising Conversions* and *An Account of the Revival of Religion in Northampton 1740–1742*). Edwards's ministry was instrumental in America's First Great Awakening, and his legacy of faithful ministry endures today. The question Edwards asked is the same one we are asking, or *ought to be asking*, right now: What are the signs that a genuine move of God is taking place?

What, in other words, are the true evidences of Spiritual fruitfulness?*

We will examine these metrics in the next chapter, but first, let's begin right where Edwards began. Edwards prefaced his list of "distinguishing marks" with a list of things that may or *may not* be signs

---

* In the rest of this book, I have decided to capitalize the word *Spiritual* when in reference to a particular outworking of the Holy Spirit to distinguish it from the generic "spirituality" we often use synonymously with "religion."

of a genuine move of God. It's a curious collection, including things like charismatic experiences, the stirring up of emotions, and the fiery preaching of hell. Edwards presented us with this list, saying that these things might be good things in many instances, but they do not themselves authenticate a work of God. A work of God may have charismatic experiences, stirring up of emotions, and the like, but it also may not. He also listed negative things, like errors and counterfeits, that do not necessarily disprove a work of God, since a genuine move of God is likely to have Satan actively trying to derail it.

It can be beneficial to apply Edwards's strong reasoning to the ecclesiological landscape today. What are the signs of actual fruitfulness? And how do we know our church is a growing part of something God is blessing? Let's look at some things that may or may not accompany a genuine move of God, what we can call *marks of neutrality*.

The first mark of neutrality is *a steady accumulation of decisions or responses during Sunday invitations*. We have all seen pastors touting their weekly "catch" on social media. Many people in these churches hear the gospel and genuinely respond to God. But we are right to be skeptical about both the frequency and the immediacy of these declarations. For one thing, this invitational strategy has been employed by evangelicals for the last fifty years, and we still face a discernible drought of mature Christianity in the West and a steady decline in evangelical numbers.[1] The discipleship processes in many "count the hands" churches seems to end right there—with the counting. This is nothing new, however. The Victorian-era London pastor Charles Spurgeon also criticized this practice, routine even in his day:

> Some of the most glaring sinners known to me were once members of a church; and were, as I believe, led to make a profession by undue pressure, well-meant but ill-judged. Do not, therefore, consider that soul-winning is or can be secured by the multiplication of baptisms, and the swelling of the size of your church. What mean these dispatches from the battle-field? "Last night, fourteen souls were under conviction, fifteen were justified,

and eight received full sanctification." I am weary of this public bragging, this counting of unhatched chickens, this exhibition of doubtful spoils. Lay aside such numberings of the people, such idle pretence of certifying in half a minute that which will need the testing of a lifetime. Hope for the best, but in your highest excitements be reasonable. Enquiry-rooms are all very well; but if they lead to idle boastings, they will grieve the Holy Spirit, and work abounding evil.[2]

Remember, Spurgeon was not only a hyperactive evangelist; he was the pastor of one of the original megachurches. Understand that he is not criticizing the act of counting, nor is he criticizing the practice of calling for responses to the gospel. He's simply urging us to go deeper. People coming to know Christ is always a good thing, no matter what kind of church they're in and no matter how they hear the gospel. But the "effectiveness" of the gospel message does not sanctify any and every evangelistic method. A simple counting of "decisions" does not prove genuine fruitfulness. A genuine decision is itself the first tiny bud of life that will one day ripen into fruit.

Second, *don't put your faith in large attendance numbers.* It wearies me to repeat this, but because American evangelicals love bigness, we must keep saying it: having a lot of people coming to your church is not a sign of faithfulness. It is a neutral sign. A lot of people coming to a church can be a good thing, of course. There is nothing inherently wrong with a big church! But there is nothing inherently right about it either. Some of the largest churches in North America are churches where you rarely hear the message of Christ crucified preached. The Mormons have big churches, but they do not adhere to Christian doctrine. We need only look to the political realm to know that a lot of people supporting something does not mean they're all heading in the right direction.

The same is true of small churches. Again, Spurgeon is helpful. He commended the practice of counting and suggested that those who are against counting are, very often, fearful they will be found lacking in their faithfulness. There's nothing noble or intrinsically holy about a small church or a stalled church. If your church isn't growing numerically, it may mean you're doing something wrong. Only a deluded minister would think it necessarily means he's doing something right!

The size of your church is a neutral matter because out of all the exhortations in the New Testament Epistles, "Get bigger" doesn't appear among them. Paul never asks the Galatians or the Colossians, "How many you runnin'?"

This doesn't mean Paul is ambivalent about their growth. It's just not high on his priority list. Some have pointed to remarks about the growth of the church found in the book of Acts as an indication of the apostles' numeric concerns. We certainly see some explosive growth discussed here, but again, I would argue that there is no ministerial preoccupation with it. The apostles and the early church members were faithful to preach and to evangelize, and the Spirit moved to continually add to their numbers. Note also that the number passages found in Acts and elsewhere remind us of the interpretative principle, "Not everything descriptive is prescriptive." In other words, we should feel free to count, just as the early church did, but we should not assume that employing their methods will lead to the same results.

In Isaiah 6, the Lord tells the prophet Isaiah to go preach to hardhearted people. Extrapolating from Isaiah's context, this would include both the churched and the unchurched. And what was the promised result of his preaching? The result, the Lord says, will be that ninety percent of his audience will fall away. In this case, God promises Isaiah a radical decline in numbers. The decline is just as much a move of God as a radical increase might be.

Jesus himself felt the sting of decrease in his ministry. In John 6, we find him meeting the felt needs of the crowd of five thousand. He miraculously feeds them all fish sandwiches. I've heard some church leaders use Jesus's miracles as a rationale for attractional ministry, but I find it an odd point to make, because as soon as Jesus starts preaching, the crowds abandon him. If this happened today, we would take Jesus aside and encourage him to redirect his giftings toward the kitchen ministry. We like our preachers a bit more . . . magnetic.

My point is that Jesus *repelled* just as many as he *attracted*. And he did not base his ministry efforts on drawing the big crowds. When we come to the end of his earthly ministry, his closest disciples were one fewer than when they started—a net loss. In 1996, I attended the Willow Creek Church Leadership Conference and recall hearing Bill Hybels say, "The core you start with will not be the core you finish with." This was certainly true for Jesus!

Look, I understand—all pastors want their churches to grow. You'd be strange if you didn't. We *all* want to reach more people and see more people transformed by the life-changing message of the gospel. But we cannot manipulate our metrics to baptize unbiblical ambitions. We cannot read the results backward to justify our presuppositions. That's pragmatism. Having a big church doesn't automatically mean you're healthy. Spurgeon would say it might just be that you're swollen (like a boil, for instance).

The Bible does not measure spiritual health in terms of size. It's not about bigness. It's largely about transformed character. In his chapter on metrics in the book *Ministry Mantras*, Pastor Bob Hyatt writes, "How many people show up on a Sunday is about the least important thing we can count, and least likely to tell us how we are maturing as a community."[3] While large attendance can tell us something, it doesn't tell us everything. And it doesn't even tell us the most important thing.

Third, *don't equate success or fruitful ministry with people having emotional experiences.* Church worship today is now effectively synonymous with music. It has become a cottage industry in the United States, something to be produced, packaged, and marketed. This music is widely accessible outside the context of a church gathering, and even *in* the context of a church gathering, it is often executed in a way that caters to our individualistic, consumeristic impulses.

Think of the different ways an attractional church might describe their worship music: exciting, vibrant, electric, dynamic, and relevant. Words like these fill postcard mailers and church websites. But why do we choose words like this to describe our music? There's certainly nothing to be gained by being boring, lifeless, and irrelevant. But is that all that's happening here? Or is there something else behind these buzzwords we market our worship with?

The words we use may subtly, or not so subtly, influence how we measure success. Think of how a typical churchgoer might determine whether a service was successful or not. All too often, the "success" of the service is measured by his or her experience. If you felt something good or pleasurable, the church leaders must have been doing something right. If you didn't, they have failed.

Again, I'm not making a call for dispassionate, disengaged preaching and singing. This is a warning against our implicit assumptions and against basing our standard for success on emotional responses. As I have traveled to speak at church gatherings, I've attended several student and college ministry events that emphasize experience—far more than I think is healthy. Adolescents, in particular, do not need help overvaluing their feelings. David Hertweck reflects on the emotionalism that dominates many evangelical student ministries, writing:

> I'm not against crying or emotions, and I'm certainly not against expressing emotions in church. I serve in a Pentecostal stream of Christianity. A Pentecostal against emotions is a bit of an oxymoron. But I am concerned about emotional experiences and hyped-up events being a primary indicator of healthy youth ministry. To reiterate, I'm not anti-crying. I'm anti-measuring impact based solely on how many tears I can crank out of a group of teenagers. . . .
>
> Many teenagers evaluate spiritual growth and the work of the Spirit based solely on how they felt during the service. You've probably heard these comments from teenagers in your youth group about the last big event they attended:
>
> "The speaker was so funny—he made me laugh a lot."
> "The band was so amazing—I loved the drummer!"
> "There's nothing like singing with so many teenagers!"
> "The videos they showed were so cool."

"The energy in the room was incredible!"

"I've never experienced anything like that."

"I wish I could stay here."

"I cried a lot."

"I had a real moment." . . .

"I really felt good."

What you probably won't hear are comments describing a new or growing appreciation for Jesus or an increased awareness of the nearness of the Spirit.[4]

To be clear, it is not wrong to experience an emotional response when you encounter God through preaching and song. We should pray for this and expect it. Again, Jonathan Edwards is helpful in setting the right balance here. He offers a strong warning against denigrating the emotions in worship:

> It is no argument that a work is not of the Spirit of God that some who are the subjects of it have been in a kind of ecstasy; wherein they have been carried beyond themselves, and have had their minds transported into a train of strong and pleasing imaginations, and a kind of visions, as though they were rapt up even to heaven and there saw glorious sights.[5]

Edwards reminds us that true worship engages worshipers on an emotional level. It would be strange if a genuine love of Jesus *failed* to make human beings feel something. Yet Edwards still lists the engagement of emotions as a neutral sign. Feelings tell us something. But they are not a reliable indication of Spiritual fruit in and of themselves. Edwards says, "We cannot conclude that persons are under the influence of the true Spirit because we see such effects upon their bodies, because this is not given as a mark of the true Spirit [in the Bible]."[6] Let's take care that the adjectives we use to describe our worship do not communicate that the worship is really for the worshiper. It's not the experience of worship that the worshiper is worshiping.

It's good when people get emotional in church. But that is not in itself a sign that your church is doing something right. As Spurgeon says, "[It is not] soul-winning, dear friends, merely to create excitement."[7]

Accumulating decisions. Large attendance. Emotional experiences. All can be good things. All can be bad things. None of these things tells us the most important things.

If these aren't the metrics that ultimately matter, which metrics are?

LifePoint Begins Interpreting the Dream

"So, what's the prize?" Felix asked. "If all this time we've been aiming the wrong direction, which way is the right one?"

You could always count on Felix Garza to cut to the chase.

Josh said, "I'm not entirely sure we've been aiming the wrong direction. In fact, I just think we don't know. We could be doing everything right. I just don't want to assume. I think we make a lot of assumptions about how well we're doing simply by doing the easy thing."

"Which is?"

"Examining our growth curve and comparing our attendance to churches around us," Josh said. "It could be that we are where we are because we're healthy. But I don't think we really know if we're healthy or not."

Matt the creative arts guy finally chimed in, somewhat meekly: "Does it really matter?"

"Does it matter?" Josh repeated, somewhat surprised by the statement.

Matt quickly tried to clarify: "I mean, if we're growing and people are happy, doesn't that tell us what we need to know? If it's not broke, don't fix it, or whatever."

"And if it's not broke," Felix added, "don't break it."

The team laughed, including Josh.

"Look, guys," Josh said, "I'm not saying I have all the answers.

I just want to start asking different questions. We don't have to get rid of the old ones. I just want to know more. Don't you?"

Children's ministry director Sandy finally weighed in: "I do."

"Thank you!" Josh said, feeling oddly vindicated.

"I mean," Sandy said, "I think about this a lot. What we're teaching the kids, how we're leading them to have a relationship with Jesus. They're asking different questions than kids were ten, twenty years ago, I think. And I wonder about how they're being taught and led at home, if what we do here on Sundays has that big of an impact. Sometimes I think . . ."

"Say it," Josh prodded.

"Sometimes I feel like we're just entertaining them."

"They're kids," Matt said, as if that needed no explanation.

Drake the youth pastor's brow furrowed. He shook his head but said nothing. He and Matt were the youngest leaders on the team, but they rarely saw eye to eye.

"Yes, they're kids," Sandy continued, "but they won't always be. I worry we aren't preparing them for the future."

Felix once again redirected: "I'm not sure if you planned on accomplishing something concrete in this meeting, Josh, and I'm afraid what we're getting into is just a round of what-if's and, if we're not careful, complaints. About church. And maybe about each other."

"Well, I'm certainly not trying to do that," Josh said. "But I do think we should give everyone the freedom to assess the ministry and their part of it openly and honestly. I hoped my questions would free up the rest of you to ask questions of your own. You asked what prize we ought to have our eyes on? I'm honestly open to suggestions. I just know the dream I had when I planted this church with my friends, and it wasn't necessarily bad. But after twenty-two years, it still seems out of reach. In fact, I'm figuring out that I don't think it will ever be reached. It's always been a moving target—just reaching more. No matter how many you attract, there's always more." He pointed up at Mike's 2,000 in 2005 banner. "And chasing *that* dream is getting old.

I'm not saying we should be satisfied with nobody else coming. I'm just tired of being ... successful."

It sounded weird. Several faces looked like they'd gotten a whiff of something smelly.

"Let me ask you this: How would we know if God was really at work here?"

CHAPTER 3

The Five Metrics That Matter Most

Going deeper than bodies and budgets

Like the leaders of other enterprises oriented around expansion, Christian leaders ponder the future of their ministries and want to know, "Is my system adequately designed for successful results?"

I work at a rapidly growing Baptist seminary, and many of the conversations we have in our department team meetings revolve around sustaining and enhancing growth. We aren't a church, of course, but we have a similar aim: we want to equip Christians for ministry. When certain degree programs are down, or we see a dip in total applicants compared to the year before, we want to know why. The answer may not be worrisome, but we are constantly evaluating, assessing, and—yes—counting. And we ask questions. What can we do to improve in this area? What adjustments need to be made to get us on our desired path?

But there are also those deeper questions, when things aren't answered by looking at numbers on a chart, data in a spreadsheet, or by tweaking the admissions or marketing mechanisms. Let's suppose there is relational tension among the student leaders. What if students are complaining about a particular class or professor? What if our students are getting good grades and succeeding intellectually, but they aren't growing very well *spiritually*? How would we know this? Can it be measured?

Some things in ministry take a deeper wisdom to discern or decipher. These can't simply be measured by counting heads. I would even argue that *the more important a metric is the more difficult it is to quantify*. This is one reason why Jesus appointed shepherds for his flock and not accountants.

Do shepherds count sheep? Of course they do. Counting is not unimportant. It's one sign to help a shepherd note problems with his flock. But it's a blunt measurement. More important still is feeding the sheep, protecting the sheep, and making sure the sheep are healthy. In the attractional paradigm, these values are easily reversed and feeding, protecting, and strengthening take on varying degrees of importance depending on the church—while the all-important measure of success is seeing the flock increase in size.

It's too simplistic to say, "the bigger the better," as if bigness equals health.

Seeing people make professions of faith tells you something. Seeing an increase in attendance tells you something. And seeing people respond emotionally to the worship service tells you something. But there are many ways to increase those numbers, not all of them biblical. You don't need Jesus to see these things happen. They are outward measures, but they don't tell us the why or the how behind them.

What, then, should we look for as signs of spiritual fruitfulness? Again, let's turn to Edwards. As you might guess, I happen to think Jonathan Edwards's "distinguishing marks of a work of the Spirit of God" hold up rather well.

The Metrics of Grace

One of the biggest problems with simply counting bodies and budgets is that there is nothing uniquely Christian about these types of increases. Businesses grow in these ways. Cities grow in these ways. Heretical ministries grow in these ways.

It's not *always* true that healthy things grow bigger. Sometimes healthy things shrink (like me, for instance, when I'm eating right and exercising). And sometimes *un*healthy things grow (like cancer). So more important than measuring a church's size is measuring its health—its fruitfulness. What do I mean by fruitfulness? We'll examine this in greater detail shortly, but for now consider the contrast between internal and external metrics. Fruitfulness pertains to the *characteristics* or internal qualities that affect the individual or community. While external measures like bodies and dollars can help us identify these characteristics or internal qualities, they aren't sufficient in themselves to tell us if a church is healthy and fruitful. For that, we will need a new scorecard. We will need a different set of measurements. We will need the metrics of grace, which tell us not simply how *many* there are but more importantly how *healthy* those many are.

Here is Edwards's list of the deeper measurements—the characteristics of a genuine move of God's Spirit.

A Growing Esteem for Jesus Christ

The primary and overarching concern for Jonathan Edwards was the glory of Christ. Did Edwards want to see his church grow? Yes, and by God's grace it did. Did he want to have a widespread impact through his writing and teaching ministry? Yes, and by God's grace he continues to do so. But that all amounts to nothing if Jesus is not at the worshipful center of everything. As Edwards wrote in *Distinguishing Marks*,

> So if the spirit that is at work among a people is plainly observed to work so as to convince them of Christ, and lead them to him—to confirm their minds in the belief of the history of Christ as he appeared in the flesh—and that he is the Son of God, and was sent of God to save sinners; that he is the only Saviour, and that they stand in great need of him; and if he seems to beget in them higher and more honourable thoughts of him than they used to have, and to incline their affections more to him; it is a sure sign that he is the true and right Spirit.[1]

Let's note a few things about this explanation and how it fits with the larger context in Edwards's book. First, Edwards used the phrase "plainly observe" to refer to the ability to measure this quality. How plain this observation may be will likely vary from church to church. It will be more difficult to measure in a larger church, but Edwards assumed that leaders observe, listen, and watch over their flock. Leaders should be able to discern the reputation of Jesus in their church.

Edwards wasn't merely describing an appreciation for Jesus or an affiliation with Jesus. People who make initial professions of faith can be plainly observed to do that. He was not simply saying that Christians are seen to identify with Jesus. Every alleged Christian does that. Edwards was looking for growth—that Jesus "seems to beget in them higher and more honourable thoughts of him than they used to have, and to incline their affections more to him." And we should note that he was describing the real Jesus. Not an idea of Jesus. Not an image of Jesus. Not Jesus as a cheerleader, fanboy, or religious avatar. Edwards wrote, "The person to whom the Spirit gives testimony, and for whom he raises their esteem must be that Jesus who appeared in the flesh, and not another Christ in his stead; nor any mystical, fantastical Christ."[2]

It's not always possible to observe the emotional engagement of people during worship to determine if their affections for Christ have been stirred and strengthened. It could be that the *idea* of Christ made them happy. Or they might equate good feelings with spiritual strength. But grace doesn't just supply feelings. Grace supplies faith.

Is your church growing in its affection for Jesus? Is he actually more important than everything else? Don't just reflexively say yes because that's the right answer. Take time to think about it.

If you're like me, after you started thinking about this, you wanted to know how in the world you could measure this. How do you know if a church is focused on the glory of Jesus Christ above all? Let me make a few suggestions.

Start with the most visible ways you communicate. In the sermon and song, is Jesus the focal point? In the sermons you preach, is Jesus a bit player, an add-on for the invitation time, or a quotable hero?

Or does your preaching and worship promote his finished work as the only hope of mankind? Do the messages focus on the law, on giving people more things to do to get right with God, or do they delight more intently in the gospel? We'll take a closer look at how to preach in a grace-centered way in chapter 5, but for now we need to ask this question: Are our sermons giving people five things to *do*, or are we reminding them that the essential message of Christianity is something God has *done*?

Musically, is the church focused on creating an experience for people or on adoring the Creator? Do our songs tell the story of the gospel? Are we, the people, the stars of the show, or is Jesus? Does the church speak in vague generalities about hope, peace, and love without connecting them to Jesus as the embodiment of these virtues? (More on this in chapter 6.) Do the people of the church prioritize Jesus over simply doing good or knowing the right doctrine? Do the pastors exhibit high esteem of Jesus? Are they "Jesus-ey" people? (More on this in chapters 7 and 10.)

If a church is not explicitly and persistently making Jesus the focus, it is not fruitful. Conversely, if a church is making Jesus the focus explicitly and persistently, it *is* being fruitful since the ongoing worship of Jesus is an essential fruit of the new birth.

A Discernible Spirit of Repentance

"The wages of sin is death" (Rom. 6:23a). The fundamental problem for every human being is not an unmet felt need but the unkept law of God. Our primary disconnect is not between ourselves and our best lives but between our lives and our Creator. People have lots of problems, and the church can help with many of them, but if we are not helping our people comprehend, confront, and confess their sin, we are failing them.

People cannot be saved if you never talk about sin. Christ is not the satisfier of our desires *before* he is the satisfier of God's wrath. Many sermons and invitation times in attractional churches focus on satisfying desires, while avoiding any mention of our need for someone to satisfy God's judgment on sin. Failure to warn people about God's judgment is the best way to lead them into it. This danger is doubly severe if you provide a veneer of religion and spirituality that deludes people about their susceptibility to wrath, telling them that they are okay now because they've improved. But if they are not truly repentant, they have merely traded their worldly pride for a spiritual one, which is worse. Edwards wrote, "When the spirit that is at work operates against the interests of Satan's kingdom, which lies in encouraging and establishing sin, and cherishing men's worldly lusts; this is a sure sign that it is a true, and not a false spirit."[3]

As I mentioned earlier, the ironic failure of the attractional church is its embrace of the positive law ("Do these things") apart from the gospel. We trade sin avoidance for works righteousness. Although the attractional model tries to correct the old-school legalism of avoiding the negative law ("Don't do these things"), it gives the false impression that the way we improve and become better is by the positive law—a to-do list of good works. But nobody will be justified by their works. Thousands of people leave attractional churches every Sunday having been convinced they will be fine if they just work harder and do more things for God. That pleases Satan because this conviction doesn't even resemble the gospel.

Some try to correct this by overcompensating. They fill their sermons with judgment and condemnation, hoping to awaken people to the reality of sin. And this can be helpful, to an extent, if it is accompanied by the good news of grace. We cannot see how good the good news is if we don't see how bad the bad news really is. It is hard to help people repent if you never preach sin.

Is the church preaching the dangers and horrors of sin? And then, in its preaching of the gospel, is the message of grace in Jesus Christ clear? Are people responding to the Spirit's conviction and comfort with repentance? Do people own and confess their sin? Is there an air of humility about the place or an air of swagger? Are the pastors bullies? Are the people narcissists? Is appropriate church discipline practiced, gentle but direct? Is there a spirit of gossip or of transparency? Is the worship service built around production value or honest intimacy with the Lord?

Are the people good repenters? Repentance is a sign of genuine fruitfulness.

A Dogged Devotion to the Word of God

A lot of churches will say they are "Bible-based," which means they quote a few Bible verses in the sermon. If you look at their small group offerings, you'll find most of them are built around special interests, hobbies, or personal demographics. But a mark of a fruitful church is a love for God's Word. Preachers preach from it as a life-giving source of food and oxygen for spiritual growth. The people study it with determination and intensity. They believe the Word of God is sufficient and powerful and authoritative.

Edwards put it this way: "The spirit that operates in such a manner as to cause in men a greater regard to the Holy Scriptures, and establishes them more in their truth and divinity is certainly the Spirit of God."[4] In other words, Edwards said that a mark of a true move of God is a high esteem of the Scriptures. I fear this mark is missing in too many evangelical churches, including many that claim to *use* the Bible but aren't effectively esteeming it.

A couple of years ago, Andy Stanley, senior pastor of North Point Community Church in Atlanta, raised some ire in an interview with the Southern Baptist Convention's Russell Moore at the annual conference of the SBC's Ethics and Religious Liberty Commission.[5] Stanley described how he envisions an entire multiweek sermon series, viewing it as one long sermon and, as a result, he may not get to the Bible for several weeks. Of course, this raised concerns with many critics of Stanley, and it was added to a short collection of other statements he has made in the past that have led some to question his use of the Bible. Stanley (with Thomas Horrocks) then issued a formal response through *Outreach* magazine, writing in part that "my take on inerrancy is not really the issue."[6]

Stanley is right. Inerrancy isn't really the issue. At least the *formal, theoretical affirmation of inerrancy* is not the issue. We can quibble with statements that appear to undermine the Old Testament accounts of the Jericho wall, but Stanley is right in saying it is not his formal commitments that are problematic. The problem is the way he applies (or in this case, doesn't apply) them. Affirming the Bible's inerrancy is not the same as trusting its sufficiency.

There are churches across America with faith statements that declare the Bible as the very Word of God, yet on Sundays they preach as if those words are not all that important. As Pastor David Prince has said, "Affirming inerrancy in principle, while rejecting its sufficiency in practice, is like saying your wife's perfect while having an affair."[7] As James says, "Faith apart from works is dead" (James 2:26). This means, if you say you have faith, but your deeds do not show faithfulness, your faith is under question. In this case, the affirmation of inerrancy without the practical application of sufficiency is dead. If we believe the Scriptures are totally reliable, why would we obscure them? Why not share them? Why be meager with them?

An approach to teaching and preaching that minimizes the use of the Scriptures or relegates them to a less than primary role is one that functionally assumes the Bible is not living and active. It denies the power of the gospel. It treats the Bible as old and crusty, something that must be cleaned up for the crowds, softened up by our logic and understanding. When Stanley elaborates on why he saves the Bible for special occasions, he is saying that the Bible needs our help, that his words are more effective than the Bible's at reaching lost people. This is another way of saying that God's Word isn't enough.

In the *Outreach* article, Stanley and Horrocks spend several paragraphs hand-wringing over the new context of post-Christian era in America, attempting to make a case that Stanley's approach to preaching and ecclesiology is the approach best-suited for turning the spiritual tide: "I'm not sitting around praying for revival. . . . I grew up in the pray for revival culture. It's a cover for a church's unwillingness to make changes conducive to real revival."[8] Well, yes, it can be. But "not sitting around praying for revival"—apart from being a strawman—can also be a cover for a church's embrace of pragmatism. Stanley goes on to say:

> Appealing to post-Christian people on the basis of the authority of Scripture has essentially the same effect as a Muslim imam appealing to you on the basis of the authority of the Quran. You may or may not already know what it says. But it doesn't matter. The Quran doesn't carry any weight with you. You don't view the Quran as authoritative.[9]

This is an important point here. My point is not to attack Andy Stanley. Honestly, he is not the problem here. I am referencing him because he is a leading practitioner of the attractional movement, and many leaders—perhaps even a few reading this book—listen to what he and others say and seek to implement it in thousands of churches.

We must remember the *supernatural reality* that the Bible carries a supernatural weight with lost people they don't often expect it to! If we truly believed the Bible was the very Word of God, inspired by the Spirit and still cutting through to the quick, dividing joint and marrow, we wouldn't save it for special occasions. And we certainly wouldn't equate its intrinsic effectiveness with the Quran's.

Stanley says:

> I stopped leveraging the authority of Scripture and began leveraging the *authority* and *stories* of the people behind the Scripture. To be clear, I don't believe "the Bible says," "Scripture teaches," and "the Word of God commands" are incorrect approaches. But they are ineffective approaches for post-Christian people.[10]

The typical attractional approach to the Bible often puts the felt needs of the lost in the driver's seat; they have the authority. This doesn't mean our preaching shouldn't address questions and objections skeptics and doubters have. It simply means you don't let the questions move you off reliance on the gospel's power.

We all want lost people to know Jesus. We want the unsaved to be saved. We agree on this. We also want to employ whatever is actually the most effective means of accomplishing this.

Is the Word of God actually God speaking to us? Is God speaking to us actually powerful? Is this power actually what helps people get saved, grow, and treasure Jesus more and more?

If the answer to those questions is yes, then a church that does not stubbornly devote itself to the Bible, as if no other words can compare, is unhealthy and unfruitful.

An Interest in Theology and Doctrine

Another key mark of a fruitful church is people who take an interest in theology and doctrine. This can be a dangerous sign, however, if it is isolated from the others (in particular the next mark discussed below, love). An interest in theology and doctrine *alone* doesn't demonstrate healthiness. Knowledge apart from grace simply puffs up and leads to pride and arrogance (1 Cor. 8:1). But this does not make knowledge disposable.

Jesus says, "God is spirit, and those who worship him must worship in spirit and truth" (John 4:24). We must resist placing spirit and truth at odds with one another, nor should we jettison one for the other. Following Jesus's words, Edwards wrote that the work of the Spirit "operates as a spirit of truth, leading persons to truth, convincing them of those things that are true."[11] What was Edwards getting at? In listing truth as one of the signs of a genuine move of God's Spirit, Edwards's point was that the true people of God love to know the things of God.

Now, nobody likes a know-it-all. We've all encountered Christian communities where honor and applause were bestowed on whoever knew the most. The church where my family holds membership draws heavily from the student population at Midwestern Seminary, and we have more than our fair share of theology geeks running around. While on the one hand this is great, supplying us with ample human resources for teaching and preaching, we must also take special care that those without formal theological training—the nonseminary members and attenders—don't feel inundated with academic theology or intimidated by a lack of formal training. We never want to give the impression that you aren't welcome or cannot grow in Christ if you can't parse Greek, give us a biographical sketch of Anselm, or trace the history of the doctrine of the Trinity.

The answer to "salvation by education" and dry intellectualism is not the neglect of theological study. Laypeople must not leave doctrine up to pastors and professors. Remember that theology, coming from the Greek words *theos* (God) and *logos* (word), simply means "the knowledge (or study) of God." If you're a Christian, you must *by definition* know God. Christians are disciples of Jesus; they are student-followers of Jesus. The longer we follow him, the more we learn about him, and the more deeply we come to know him.

Having a mind lovingly dedicated to God is biblically required of us, most notably in the great commandment: "You shall love the Lord your God with all your heart and with all your soul and with all your *mind*" (Matt. 22:37). Loving God with all our minds means more than theological study, but it does not mean less than that.[12]

We are saved by grace alone through faith alone (Eph. 2:8) totally apart from any works of our own (Rom. 3:28), and that includes our intellectual exertions. Yet the faith by which we are justified, the faith that receives the completeness of Christ's finished work and his perfect righteousness, is a *reasonable* faith. Faith is not the same as rationality, but that does not mean our faith is irrational. The exercise of faith is predicated on information—most notably, the historical announcement of the good news of what Jesus has done—and the strengthening of our faith depends on information as well.

Our growth in the grace of God is connected closely with our pursuit of the knowledge of God's character and works as revealed in God's Word. Contrary to what modern-day idolaters of doubt teach, the Christian faith is founded on facts. Hebrews 11:1 reminds us that faith is not a leap into the dark for Christians. Instead, faith is inextricably connected to our conviction and sense of assurance. Generally speaking, the more theological facts we feast on, the greater our assurance and conviction as our faith grows and matures.

Paul tells his young protégé Timothy, "Keep a close watch on yourself and on the teaching. Persist in this, for by so doing you will save both yourself and your hearers" (1 Tim. 4:16). Here he reminds Timothy that the sanctification resulting in continual discipleship to Christ necessarily includes intense study of God's Word. Rightly executed, the study of God will authenticate and fuel the kind of worship that results in the other four distinguishing marks. True Christians do not believe in some vague God. We do not trust in spiritual platitudes. True Christians believe in the triune God of the Holy Scriptures and place their trust by the real Spirit in a real Savior—Jesus—the one proclaimed in the specific words of the historical gospel.

Knowing the right information about God is one way we authenticate our Christianity. Intentionally or consistently err in vital facts about God and you jeopardize the veracity of your claim to know God. This is why we must pursue theological understanding and knowledge, not just in our pastor's sermons but in our church's music and in our church's prayers. Spiritual growth involves deep, fundamental changes to the heart and, consequently, our behavior, leading us to seek deeply after the things of God with our minds. "Do not be conformed to this world," Paul writes, "but be transformed by the renewal of your mind, that by testing you may discern what is the will of God, what is good and acceptable and perfect" (Rom. 12:2). Transformation begins with the renewing of our minds.

Healthy, fruitful churches are made up of Christians who are searching out God's ways and following the trails of doctrine in the Scriptures straight to the throne. In our day, emotion and experience are often set at odds with the study of doctrine and theology, and churches that devote themselves to one will often keep the other at arm's length. Both extremes are unfruitful—a church that's all head knowledge without heart and a church that's all feeling without depth.

The church has not endured for two thousand years on "spiritual feelings." The grace of God empowers the church by inflaming the desires of people toward greater interest in theology and doctrine.

But how do you get there? The seeds of this are planted in

corporate worship and watered and nurtured through the process of discipleship. We'll look at this in more detail in chapter 7.

Edwards wraps up his list of distinguishing marks of a genuine move of God by emphasizing the gospel-driven fulfillment of the Great Commandment. Let's conclude with the fifth and final sign of true fruitfulness: love.

An Evident Love for God and Neighbor

A move of God's Spirit will bear the fruit of evident love for God and for our neighbor. This is exactly as it sounds. True fruitfulness is evidenced chiefly in obedience to the commands of God, the greatest of which is loving God and loving our neighbors as ourselves (Luke 10:27). If a church exists for the sake of its own survival, for the sake of its own enterprise, or for the sake of creating wonderful experiences for people, it is not fruitful, no matter how big it gets.

Fruitful churches may or *may not* see steady conversions, but they will steadily have a heart of service and compassion for the world outside their doors. In 1 John 4:12–13, the apostle John writes, "If we love one another, God abides in us and his love is perfected in us. By this we know that we abide in him and he in us, because he has given us of his Spirit." In other words, a distinguishing mark of God's Spirit growing a church is a growing in love. Edwards put it this way:

> In these verses love is spoken of as if it were that wherein the very nature of the Holy Spirit consisted; or, as if divine love dwelling in us, and the Spirit of God dwelling in us were the same thing. . . . Therefore, this last mark which the apostle gives of the true Spirit he seems to speak of as the most eminent: and so insists much more largely upon it than upon all the rest.[13]

The first way this love is made evident is through the way Christians love one another. As a church grows larger this may be more difficult to track and observe. People loving a great program is not the same as people loving each other. To accurately diagnose the quality and disposition of relationships requires an engaged leadership, invested pastoral care, and wise spiritual discernment.

It's often easier to diagnose the love of the church corporately for its neighbors in the community. Love requires knowledge, awareness, and sacrificial devotion to the needs of others. Are the leaders aware of their surroundings? Does the church operate almost as an island in a sea of outsiders? Do you feel like you're in a bubble?

If your church closed tomorrow, would the neighborhood care? Take some time to wrestle with that question. If your church does not have relationships with those outside the church body and leaves little mark in the community, it may not be a fruitful church.

We've come to the end of Jonathan Edwards's list of distinguishing marks of a genuine move of God's Spirit. The checklist is as daunting as it is concise, isn't it? I refer to these marks as "the metrics of grace," and I've chosen that term for three reasons: (1) measuring this way requires going deeper than fleshly measurements, to a place only grace can take us; (2) getting healthy in these ways requires being empowered the way only grace empowers us; and (3) applying these marks requires a courageous self-evaluation through which only grace can secure us.

Measuring the Spirit

At this point, you may be thinking to yourself: "These things aren't easy to measure. How are we supposed to do this?" The metrics of grace are harder to quantify than simply counting hands and bodies. I think this is one reason why we tend to equate hands raised and bodies in seats with fruitfulness. But those metrics may lead us to miss a genuine work of God's Spirit. Consider this: Can a church be Spiritually fruitful without seeing many or frequent conversions, without bursting at the seams in attendance, without creating "worship experiences" that stir people emotionally and imaginatively? These can be good things when they're done for biblical reasons and to honor God. But they are not themselves indicators of genuine fruit.

Yes, the early church counted. It's fine to count. But the biblical marker of success is never high attendance or a focus on decision-producing. That doesn't exist in the pages of the New Testament. What we see is faithfulness. And out of that faithfulness we sometimes see fruit, arriving "in season," and other times we do not, when fruit is "out of season" (2 Tim. 4:2). The church is not called to be successful by attaining certain numbers or meeting a preset standard of growth, but we are called to be faithful. And that faithfulness will lead to fruitful growth. There may be seasons—hopefully many!—when your fruit leads to numeric growth. But the fruit of faithfulness, according to the Bible, is deeper discipleship, maturing in Christ, and a more loving reach outward in service to our neighbors. There may be times when this fruit and numeric success go hand in hand, but that is no ready guarantee for faithfulness.

What we need is a new scorecard.

Commenting on 1 Thessalonians 3:12–4:12, Pastor Mark Dever writes,

> You see, again here, you have the idea of growth. He says, "as in fact you are living," do this "more and more." He doesn't just want them to abide, but to abound. The mark of a growing Christian isn't perfection, but it's the desire to grow more.
>
> Paul *urges* them to do this. This word "urge" in v. 1 is a word Paul used to introduce passionate exhortations, to seize the point and to drive it home. "Brothers, we instructed you how to live in order to please God, as in fact you are living. Now we ask you and urge you in the Lord Jesus to do this more and more." More and more, Paul urged them to grow in living-so-as-to-bring-pleasure-to-God. *This* is the motive of a growing church.[14]

I know that many of you are nodding your heads, thinking, "Okay, this all sounds great, but how do we *actually* measure these things?" What questions can we ask that might help us get beneath the surface and better understand the health of our church? Is there a process that we can follow that will help us get at the "more and more"?

I'm glad you asked! Throughout this book I'll provide questions for you to answer and discuss, questions that can help you discern where you are at and determine if you are seeing biblical fruit. These are questions a church leadership team can talk about, but they are also great for those attending a church to think about, especially as an exhortation to realign with God's mission. Here are just a few diagnostic questions to help you begin "measuring" your church and the spiritual growth of its people:

1. Are those being baptized continuing to walk in the faith years down the line?
2. Do we have a clear way of discipling people? Why or why not?
3. How many of the attendees of the worship gathering participate in community groups? If the percentage is small, what are some reasons for this?
4. Can our members articulate the gospel? How would we go about finding this out?
5. If we asked ten people in our community who do not attend our church to describe what they think of it, what would they say? If the church shut down tomorrow, would our community care?

How you answer these questions will vary from church to church, but it will require a level of engagement and a system of care that goes deeper than counting. Yes, it will take work, but this is what we are called to as leaders. The growth of your people and the endurance of your ministry are more than worth the additional time and energy.

LifePoint Reconsiders Results

"How would we know if God was really at work here?" Josh asked. "Just because we're happy doesn't mean everybody else is. And even if everybody else is, that doesn't mean *God* is."

That got the team's attention.

"So here's where I think we should start," Josh said. "Fearless inventory. This won't answer everything, but it will go a lot further than we're going now. I want to survey our church—as many members and regular attenders as we can. I'll leave it to you guys to figure out how to get it implemented, but here are the questions it should ask . . ."

Josh stood and approached the white board, blue dry-erase marker in hand. He uncapped it with a flourish that made Sandy giggle.

"We'll start with the basics: age range, marital status, area of town. Then we want to know if they're a member or an attender. Then we want to know how they would describe themselves: not yet a Christian, a new Christian—say, less than three years—or a Christian of more than three years. Maybe add a 'not sure' option. That could be helpful."

Pastor Rob asked, "Isn't that somewhat redundant to ask if someone is a member and then if they are not a believer? Our members are believers."

Josh looked at him, not really smiling, not really frowning. "Are they?"

Rob reclined into his seat back as if he'd been blown back by the wind.

Josh continued, "I want to know where people are. It's possible we have members who aren't quite sure about their faith right now. Or who slipped through the cracks of our membership process for whatever reason."

Felix cocked his head to the side on that comment. The membership process fell under his leadership area.

Josh stopped and put the marker to his chin, thinking. "What else?" he asked.

Rob said, "What about spiritual disciplines?"

"Yes! Good. Let's find out how often they read the Bible and pray. Give several frequency options to choose from."

Drake jumped in: "How about questions that go beyond their membership status, like how often they attend? If it's possible we have members who aren't believers, it's possible we have members who don't attend all that often."

"Or," Rob added, "attenders who have been here every Sunday for years but for some reason aren't members."

"That's true," Josh said. "How about community group involvement?"

"What would be interesting," Rob replied, "would be to see how many say they regularly attend community group and then compare that with the actual attendance numbers from my group leaders."

"Ask about serving in the church," Sandy said, "or even in the community."

The team made a few more suggestions. Discussion ensued. Some questions were deemed too nuanced, others not incredibly significant. Josh was reluctant to make the survey too long. In the end, he added a final question:

"How would you describe your current rate of spiritual growth? With these options: growing a little, growing a lot, not growing, not sure."

In all, they settled on ten questions, which Josh had listed on the white board. The team sat there and stared at it for a minute before Felix finally said, "What you're suggesting we do is not a solution."

Josh sat down and pulled up to the table. "What do you mean?"

"Well," Felix continued, "I don't mean it's not the right thing to do. I just mean that if you gauge the health of everybody in this place, assuming everybody tells the truth and you get an accurate representation, that still doesn't tell you what to do about it. I know I'm always thinking about keeping things running—"

"And running smoothly," Rob, the pastor for growth, added.

"Right. And running smoothly. But you know as well as I do that a diagnosis is not a cure. If we get the results you suspect we might get, what should we do about it?"

"I don't know," Josh said.

"Forgive me, Pastor," Felix said, "but that hardly seems good enough. If you open up this can of worms, you will need to contain them somehow. Because once we get this survey out there, people will want to know what it's for. We need to know what to tell them, if anything, and be as specific as possible. And if you're right that everything we've been doing hasn't been achieving the results we think it has, we need to figure out what will."

Josh liked that Felix said *we*, not *you*.

"Felix, first of all, I love you, man. Second, I'm beginning to think that what we need *isn't* a different way of doing church to achieve results. It's that we probably need a different way of doing church period. We need to make sure whatever we're doing, we're doing because it's what God has called us to do."

Felix shrugged. The idea of doing things and not being concerned about results was not his forte.

"But," Josh added, "like Bob said earlier: we can figure it out together. Okay?"

"Sure," Felix said, but he didn't sound convinced.

"So . . . how soon can we get the survey up and running?"

CHAPTER 4

Putting the Gospel in the Driver's Seat

Repurposing your church around Spiritual power

Are you sitting down?"

Felix Garza was just being silly. Josh was already sitting down. In fact, he was stuffing his face with nachos. Pastors Rob and Bob had joined them at their favorite Tex-Mex joint so Felix could share the results of the survey. It had taken them a week to put it together, and they'd provided a secure link to every contact email they had on file for persons connected to the church. They gave people three weeks to complete it, pushed along by copious announcements. Six weeks later, the results were in.

Felix wanted to put together some infographics to help everybody get a better grasp on the data, but they would wait until the presentation to the whole team. The pastoral team was getting the sneak preview, mainly so they could figure out how Josh might be able to present it, in case the results were overly negative.

"Let me have it," Josh said, picking a jalapeno off his plate and popping it into his mouth. Then, chewing, "Don't hold back."

"Okay. Rather than try to set anything up, I'll just read you the bullet points."

Rob pushed his own plate aside to make room for his notebook. He watched Felix expectantly over his pen, poised to record everything.

Felix began: "We had just a little over 2,000 respondents, which is interesting because after three weeks of begging people to complete the survey, there are literally hundreds of attenders who did not. Exactly 2,124 people submitted the form. The vast majority of those who responded say they've been a Christian for more than three years—that figure was, specifically, 1,808. Of the 316 remaining, 299 have been Christians less than three years."

"Hmm," Bob said.

"What, Bob?" Josh replied.

"Nothing. I just wouldn't have thought that. I thought we'd have a lot more new Christians at LifePoint."

"Interestingly enough," Felix continued, "Seventeen people said they weren't sure where they stood spiritually."

"How many identified as 'not a Christian yet'?" Rob asked.

"Zero."

"What?"

"Yep. Zero."

"No unbelievers?"

Felix said, "Now, it could be for several reasons. Maybe it's mostly unbelievers among the hundreds that didn't take the survey. Maybe they misunderstood and thought it was just for 'church people.' Or maybe people were uncomfortable identifying with that particular word. Maybe if we'd put *seeker* or something like that the results would be different. If they're an unbeliever attending our church and taking this survey seemed a fine thing to do, they may be inclined to want to identify as part of the group, you know? So, if they aren't really sure or are still sorting things out spiritually, they could have just marked the new Christian field as a kind of good faith choice, an act of optimism. Remember this isn't scientific."

"No, you're right," Josh said. "Not scientific. But given that nearly everybody identified as an 'older' Christian, it does tell us something *generally* about who we're reaching. What else you got?"

"Here's something I found interesting," Felix said. "Roughly half of the respondents identified as members—1,048."

"Whoa," Rob said.

"Exactly. We don't have nearly that many members on the books. I checked the roster, and as of last December when we held the last membership class, we have a total of 624 members."

"Why would 400 extra people identify as members?" Bob asked.

Rob answered, "Probably because they have no idea what a member is. They attend regularly, and maybe have for years, so they feel like members of the church. They probably don't equate it with a class and an assigned volunteer role—just a feeling of being 'a part' of the group, a sense of belonging."

Felix said, "That's my guess too. And I guess I need to own that, that we've done a poor job communicating membership to our church. But what's even more interesting is how many newer Christians identified as members versus 'more than three years' Christians. Newer Christians identified as church members at nearly the same rate as older Christians."

Josh puzzled. "Help me out."

"Well, I have no way of knowing which 624 are telling the truth about their membership because the survey was anonymous. I have IP addresses, but no names. That's even assuming all 624 members are actually included in the 1,048 who think they're members. But . . . if I had to guess at an interpretation, it would be this: the newer somebody is in the faith or to our church, the more they feel like they belong. The longer someone is here, the less so."

Rob said, "I'm not surprised by that at all."

Josh placed his hands on the table on either side of his plate. He wasn't happy. But like Rob, he also wasn't surprised. He said gently, "Rob, I want to hear more from you on that later. See if we're on the same page. But first, Felix, thank you for all this. You and your team did an awesome job. But before we start thinking through how to present this to the rest of the leadership team, give me your thirty-thousand-foot appraisal. Button it up for me like you're so good at."

Felix put the file folder with the results in his lap. "This process was a lot more insightful than I thought it would be—no offense—but

I think if I had to sum it all up, the two biggest takeaways for how we do church are these: One, we aren't reaching unbelievers like we think we are. And two, we aren't growing believers like we think we are. In fact, we have probably radically miscalculated our success on both fronts."

Reconnecting with the Supernaturality of Christianity

Paul writes in 2 Corinthians 3:1–6,

> Are we beginning to commend ourselves again? Or do we need, as some do, letters of recommendation to you, or from you? You yourselves are our letter of recommendation, written on our hearts, to be known and read by all. And you show that you are a letter from Christ delivered by us, written not with ink but with the Spirit of the living God, not on tablets of stone but on tablets of human hearts.
>
> Such is the confidence that we have through Christ toward God. Not that we are sufficient in ourselves to claim anything as coming from us, but our sufficiency is from God, who has made us sufficient to be ministers of a new covenant, not of the letter but of the Spirit. For the letter kills, but the Spirit gives life.

The gospel is always an interruption. It interrupts our lives, our sinful habits, our selfishness and rebellion, redirecting our attention away from ourselves to God and his work and Word. Sometimes the gospel even interrupts our ways of "doing church."

In our day, when consumerism and pragmatism are widespread, our human ideas need a supernatural hijacking by the supernatural gospel. The Christian church is unlike other organizations. It is a movement arriving from, begun by, sustained in, and heading toward heaven itself. Real Christianity cannot be reduced to methods and ordinary human metrics. It must always allow for the supernatural.

The great Princeton theologian B. B. Warfield concurs:

The religion of the Bible is a frankly supernatural religion. By this is not meant merely that, according to it, all men, as creatures, live, move and have their being in God. It is meant that, according to it, God has intervened extraordinarily, in the course of the sinful world's development, for the salvation of men otherwise lost.[1]

Even successful churches need extraordinary intervention. God is in the business of interrupting our "normal" Christianity.

So how do we extricate ourselves and our churches from the spirit of consumerism and pragmatism that has infected the church and reclaim the essence of biblical Christianity? What we need is to repent of decades of relying upon pragmatic methodology and materialist theology and to reclaim the proclamation of the gospel of Jesus Christ as the power of salvation for anybody, anywhere, anytime. The United States, in particular, desperately needs churches to recommit to the *countercultural supernaturalism* of biblical Christianity. This entails a greater commitment to rely on the Spirit working through his prescribed mean, not ours.

To be clear, our creativity and intelligence can certainly adorn the gospel of grace, but no amount of creativity and intelligence can awaken a dead soul. Sacrificial good works and biblical social justice can affirm the power and truth of the good news, but neither can awaken a dead soul. Only the foolishness of the gospel (1 Cor. 1:18), the good news that God forgives sin in Christ and transforms sinners by grace, can do that. As Western culture grows increasingly post-Christian, more churches become ashamed of the foolishness of the gospel. It is not a message that appeals to worldly wisdom or offers a path to worldly success. But the apostle Paul knows that the hope of the church and world is not found in personal or corporate success, in the standards of this world, but in the alien righteousness of Christ. He announces the powerful hope of this scandalous historical headline and contrasts it with worldly wisdom: "For Christ did not send me to baptize but to preach the gospel, and not with words of eloquent wisdom, lest the cross of Christ be emptied of its power" (1 Cor. 1:17).

Paul knows that all too often our creativity and intelligence don't adorn the gospel but obscure it. In some church environments they may unwittingly replace it. But the apostle encourages us not to be ashamed—intentionally or even unintentionally—of the gospel, for it is the power of salvation given to us to steward. *There is nothing else.* "I decided to know nothing among you except Jesus Christ and him crucified" (1 Cor. 2:2).

One of the most frequent temptations pastors and church leaders face today is to replace a steady commitment to gospel preaching and revival prayer with human ingenuity and industriousness. Can these coexist? Certainly. But we must also guard against allowing ourselves to replace the work that only the Holy Spirit can do. The Holy Spirit can do far more than we think or ask, and his timing may not always follow our goals or fit our plans. But let's not run ahead of him.

The church must return to Christian supernaturalism. How do we do this?

Recover the Supernaturality of Prayer

You probably expect me to mention prayer at some point. Before you tune out the next few paragraphs, thinking, "I've heard this before, and I know prayer is important," I want you to be honest with yourself. Are you a man or woman of prayer? Is prayer a defining mark of your church?

Prayer is expressed helplessness. When we're not engaged in prayer, it's because we feel like "we got this." The extent to which you are not engaged in prayer is the extent to which you are relying on your own strength. I know many churches have plans, strategies, vision, books, workshops, consultants, and rely on their creativity. All those things are good things, but good things can also be barriers to God's ways. It's possible that our reliance on these things prevents us from being filled by the Spirit.

In many evangelical churches today, the doctrinal statement of faith could easily be modified to affirm a belief in the Father, the Son, and holy ingenuity. The constant temptation is to replace reliance upon the Spirit with our best efforts blessed by God. But if the Holy Spirit is not at work among us, we have nothing. The more we push prayer out of our planning, preparation, and production, the more we quench the Holy Spirit's work, frustrating the greater work God may want to accomplish through our humble dependence.

Ezekiel 37 ought to make us nervous. In it, the prophet receives a vision of a valley of dry bones. During the vision Ezekiel sees the bones begin to rattle and animate, but they are not yet alive. Ezekiel says, "And I looked, and behold, there were sinews on them, and flesh had come upon them, and skin had covered them. But there was no breath in them" (37:8). This suggests that a church can *look* alive and yet not *be* alive. Or consider Jesus's warning to the Sardisian church in Revelation 3:1: "I know your works. You have the reputation of being alive, but you are dead." This is a Christian church, known for its good works with a reputation for health, but in the eyes of Jesus, it is dead. Ezekiel 37 and Revelation 3:1 are sobering reminders for church leaders who have megachurch dreams.

May we never mistake our busyness and bigness for the breath of God.

The Holy Spirit does not always follow our formulas. "The wind blows where it wishes, and you hear its sound, but you do not know where it comes from or where it goes. So it is with everyone who is born of the Spirit" (John 3:8). In preaching Acts 2:43 ("and awe came upon every soul"), my friend Ray Ortlund said, "That's not something you can put in the worship bulletin: '10:00 a.m. worship in song. 10:30 a.m. awe comes down.'"

The Holy Spirit's power cannot be conjured or manipulated by us. And the kind of power only he can bring cannot be produced or fabricated by us. So we express our utter dependence on him to do what we need done by our practical commitment to the antipragmatism of prayer. We honor the Spirit with our reliance, not with our self-centered know-how.

Let's bathe our services in prayer. Let's bathe our sermons in prayer. "We are [not] sufficient in ourselves to claim anything as coming from us, but our sufficiency is from God" (2 Cor. 3:5).

Everybody in the Bible who thought they had what it takes apart from the Spirit ended up crashing and burning.

We'll return to the importance of prayer in chapter 6, but for now I'd encourage you to let the words from Maurice Roberts's sermon "Prayer for Revival" be your prayer as well:

> It is to our shame that we have imbibed too much of this world's materialism and unbelief. What do we need more than to meditate on the precious covenant promises of Holy Scripture until our souls have drunk deeply into the spirit of a biblical supernaturalism? What could be more profitable than to eat and drink of heaven's biblical nourishment till our souls become vibrant with the age-old prayer for revival, and till we find grace to plead our suit acceptably at the throne of grace?
>
> The Lord has encouraged us to hope in him still. O that he would teach us to give him no rest day or night till he rain righteousness upon us![2]

Recover the Supernaturality of Scripture

When Willow Creek examined the results of its REVEAL study, diagnosing the spiritual life of their congregation, they found that fewer people were maturing than they expected. Among the community members who had identified as "growing in their faith," they wanted to dig in further to know what was making the difference. Do you know what they discovered? The number one catalyst for spiritual growth was Bible study.

> Nothing else even comes close to having the same impact as the Bible when it comes to spiritual growth. For those in the Close to Christ and Christ-Centered stages, reflection on Scripture is twice as impactful as any other catalyst. The key difference

in the impact of reflection on Scripture across the spiritual continuum is frequency. For someone in the Exploring Christ stage, shifting from reflecting on Scripture rarely (a few times per year) to frequently (several times per week) speeds the movement to the Growing in Christ stage. For the later movements, increasing from frequent to daily reflection on Scripture plays a significant role in spiritual growth.[3]

The American Bible Society has done their own surveys and found the same results: the number one predictor of spiritual growth is "engaging Scripture."[4] Numerous other researchers and studies have found the same thing. If we are looking for the one thing that effects change in the human heart, nothing compares to the Word of God. This shouldn't surprise us. The Bible claims as much about itself: "For the word of God is living and active, sharper than any two-edged sword, piercing to the division of soul and of spirit, of joints and of marrow, and discerning the thoughts and intentions of the heart" (Heb. 4:12). And Isaiah 55:11 tells us that God's Word will not "return unto me void" (KJV). But if all this is true, why do we ration out Bible verses in our teaching, using as little as possible? Do we believe our words more reliable, more powerful, more authoritative than the Bible's?

Preachers, this is one you need to wrestle with. Having preached weekly to a congregation myself, and now as a traveling speaker, I know the constant pressure there is to communicate timeless truths in timely ways. The drive to be creative, to be engaging, to be relevant, and to be inspiring is always there. And yet, if we do not speak to others primarily from the desire to proclaim the Bible, we are wasting our time. And theirs too.

If the Bible really is God's Word, and God's Word really is powerful, let's treat it as more important than our words and our abilities.

Recover the Supernaturality of the Gospel

"The letter kills," Paul says in 2 Corinthians 3:6. In verse 7, he calls it "the ministry of death." He goes on to say that what really transforms people is the glory of Jesus Christ. This culminates in verse 18, where he says, "We all, with unveiled face, beholding the glory of the Lord, are being transformed into the same image from one degree of glory to another."

The Bible has a supernatural power to address the human condition. Within the Bible is an essential message with the power to draw our focus to Jesus Christ and transform our hearts. This gospel is the power of God. It's supernatural. Let's dig into what this means for the church.

Repurposing the Church through Recentering on the Gospel

Let me play my hand, if you haven't seen it already. My goal in this book is to convince you that your church and its slate of programs and ministries—no matter how successful they have been in attracting people—should be centered on the good news of the finished work of Jesus Christ. The attractional model cannot be the foundation for your methods and programs. It must give way to the gospel because the gospel is where the power of God is manifest. The gospel swallows up our pragmatic paradigms like a white dwarf swallows planets. Pragmatism has a place, but it's not at the center. We must be gospel centered.

First, I'll clarify what the gospel *is*. Because many people express this message in many ways (not all of them wrong), and because there is a "gospel-centered" movement in American Christianity today, there is a danger that the word *gospel* becomes a fuzzy buzzword or the shibboleth of a particular evangelical tribe. We should aim for clarity and define what we mean. So what is the gospel?

The word *gospel*, from the Greek word *evangelion*, means "good news." The gospel refers to the good news that God sent his Son Jesus to live a sinless life, die a substitutionary death, and rise from the dead so that sinners who repent and trust in Jesus will be forgiven and have eternal life. We can expand this or shorten it, but this is a basic summation of the message we are called to share with others.

Notice that the gospel is not something we do but something that is done by the triune God—Father, Son, and Spirit working together on mission to redeem sinful, rebellious humanity and establish God's kingdom on earth as it is in heaven. It is, as the word suggests, *news*—a newspaper headline. It is a historical fact with ongoing significance for the present. We do not "do" or "be" the gospel; we respond to it.

A problem arises in the church when we think of the gospel as exclusively for lost people who do not yet know Jesus. We embrace the gospel as the content of our evangelism and mission, but we do not see how it applies to those who have accepted Christ. Why would Christians need the gospel if they already have it? If they didn't have it, they wouldn't be Christians! I once had a pastor say this very thing to me. I was commending the practice of gospel-centered preaching, where the message points people to Jesus and the application is rooted in responding to what Jesus has done for us, and he said, "Jared, my church already *has* the gospel. They need something else right now."

What he meant was that his church didn't need to be reminded of something they already knew, they needed *practical* help in everyday Christian living. What does the gospel have to do with that?

As it turns out, quite a bit.

Many churches tend to operate this way, as if the gospel is past tense for the Christian and present tense only for the seeker or unbeliever. Once you get the gospel, you have it, and then it's time to move on to deeper things. But the gospel isn't Christianity 101—it's the entire degree program.

Hopefully, we have some clarity on the gospel now, but you may still want to know what it means for a church to "center" on the gospel. A gospel-centered church is one that explicitly and intentionally connects its teaching, programs, ministry philosophy, and mission to the content of the gospel. As my friend Joel Lindsey has written, "A gospel-centered church is so because the gospel is the engine that propels its mission. . . . The gospel is the primary lens through which to view the world and the people and things in it."[5] In other words, the gospel isn't just a fad or style you lay over your philosophy of ministry—something traditional, something Baptist, something Reformed—as if "gospel-centrality" were an Instagram filter for your church. The gospel of Jesus Christ should inform, influence, and drive everything we do.

Why should we center our churches on the gospel? Because the Bible says the gospel is central, effectual, and versatile.

The Bible Says the Gospel Is Central

Paul tells us flat-out that nothing is more important than the gospel. It's of "first importance" and should have top billing in the church: "For I delivered to you as *of first importance* what I also received: that Christ died for our sins in accordance with the Scriptures, that he was buried, that he was raised on the third day in accordance with the Scriptures" (1 Cor. 15:3–4, emphasis added).

This message is central. It should not be placed in the background, buried in a statement of faith, saved for special occasions, or treated as an afterthought. It is to be the hallmark and centerpiece of all a church does. As Paul writes in Philippians 3:16, "Let us hold true to what we have attained." In case you think Paul is only referring to the gospel as a first step rather than something vital in the ongoing life of the church, you need only examine his letters to the churches and to his disciples Timothy and Titus. Every one of Paul's letters—to Christians in churches—begins with a gospel proclamation. The length of the proclamation usually depends on the length of the letter, but before Paul gets to the practical application and the instructions, he always reminds his Christian recipients of the centrality of the grace of God in Jesus for everything we do, personally and ecclesiologically. He does so because they are prone to forget. He does so because we are powerless to change without the gospel.

The Bible Says the Gospel Is Effectual

A second reason we want to make the gospel of Jesus Christ central in our ministry is because *only the gospel is power* (Rom. 1:16; 1 Cor. 1:18; Eph. 3:7; 1 Thess. 1:5). The good news of Jesus invites a power outside of ourselves, in spite of ourselves, sourced in the Holy Spirit himself, who is obliged and committed to furthering the glory of Jesus Christ through the proclamation of his life, death, and resurrection.

The gospel is power from heaven, and it is stewarded to us!

Do you want to see the lost saved? Do you want Christians matured? Only the gospel can empower both transformations. In Titus 2:11–12, Paul writes that the grace of God trains us to repent of our sin. In Philippians 2:12–13, he says the "working out" of our salvation is due to God "working in" us. The gospel speaks powerfully to those "near" and "far off" (Eph. 2:17).

In 2 Corinthians 3, Paul describes how even the glory of the law is outshined by the glory of Christ's gospel. He argues that the commands—think about our emphasis in preaching on steps and tips—cannot change anyone. The kind of change we want, for both lost and found, only comes from beholding the glory of Jesus (3:18).

So why would we assume people know this message? If a steady diet of steps and tips cannot change a heart, but the gospel does, why isn't the American church giving people more gospel rather than more law? Why isn't Jesus the star of our preaching?

To many people outside—and even inside—the church, what I'm encouraging us to reject has come to seem perfectly normal. The idea of abandoning a steady diet of things to do and replacing it with a regular focus on the finished work of Christ even strikes many Christians as weird. I know because I've pastored people who have struggled with hearing more about Jesus than themselves in weekly preaching and teaching. But we must press forward, renewing our commitment to good news over good advice. We must embrace the strange "newness" of this.

So here's what I propose: Let's rehitch our ministries to the supernatural power of God. Let's recover prayer, preaching the Word, and centering on the good news of the finished work of Christ. And let's see what happens.

Let's make Christianity weird again.

The Bible Says the Gospel Is Versatile

Let's return to 1 Corinthians 15, where Paul tells us that the gospel is the most important thing (v. 3). Something in the verses that precede this is radically transformative for the way we usually think of the Christian life: "Now I would remind you, brothers, of the gospel I preached to you, which you received, in which you stand, and by which you are being saved, if you hold fast to the word I preached to you—unless you believed in vain" (vv. 1–2).

In the verses that follow, Paul says that the gospel is the foundation and power for our everyday life. But notice how he sets this up. He emphasizes that they need to be reminded of the gospel, implying that they might forget it. Then he says that it is something they "received." That's past tense. Paul is referring to the conversion and profession of faith that begins the Christian life. Maybe you walked an aisle in response to an altar call. Maybe you were alone reading a Christian book or tract or watching an evangelistic message on television. Maybe a friend or relative shared the gospel with you. We come to Christ in a variety of ways, but we all get there through the gospel message. We "received" the gospel.

Paul doesn't end there. He goes on to say that those who received the gospel "stand" in the gospel—present tense. In other words, you didn't "get" the gospel, and you're all done with it now, ready to move on to bigger and better things. We stand in the gospel. Nothing is bigger and better than the gospel of grace. You need it every day. The Father lays out new mercies every morning, and following Jesus daily is rooted in him because of the gospel of union with Christ and is empowered by his Spirit because of the gospel of his indwelling presence.

In Galatians 3:3, Paul sarcastically asks the church if they think they can graduate from the gospel: "Are you so foolish? Having begun by the Spirit, are you now being perfected by the flesh?" Paul is refuting the idea that we receive the gospel (past tense) and then sustain ourselves through our good works. Rather, we are sustained by the gospel in which we stand.

Paul continues in 1 Corinthians 15, and it gets better! We don't just receive the gospel (past tense) and stand in the gospel (present tense). Paul says we are also "being saved" (15:2) by this gospel (present-future tense). This speaks of our ongoing sanctification, the way Christ's grace conforms us to his glory to make us more like him, and it speaks of

Christ's second coming, when he will deliver us from sin and present us perfect in resurrected bodies on a restored and new creation.

Past, present, future—the gospel applies at every point. This is bigger than we think.

And it's bigger still. The fear of some who consider embracing gospel-centrality is that it doesn't have legs. You might think, "There's just no way the gospel can provide a fresh word every Sunday. We need more!" But these fears are rooted in unbiblical ways of thinking about God and his grace. The gospel cannot be boring. Its implications are multidimensional and cosmic. It speaks to our individual needs and presents a comprehensive understanding of reality. Even angels long to look into the depths of the gospel (1 Peter 1:12). Because the good news is about *Jesus Christ*, to say the good news is boring is like saying Jesus is boring! To be bored by the gospel, in fact, is to enter very dangerous territory. May we never encounter the wonder, the majesty, the love, and the power of Jesus and yawn in response.

The gospel of Jesus is so simple that a child can understand it, believe it, and be saved, yet the gospel is so vast, complex, and glorious that we along with the angels will revel in it for eternity. If we cannot see how it might hold someone's attention week after week, the deficiency is with us, not with it. The gospel will preach, so preach the gospel.

You can't wear it out. You can't outperform it. You can't find anything more interesting, more powerful, or more *relevant* than the gospel. The real foolishness is *not* to center on it. The gospel will hold and sustain your church in a way all the relevant programming, applicational teaching, and worship experiences never will. As Tim Keller notes, "Because the gospel is endlessly rich, it can handle the burden of being the one 'main thing' of a church."[6]

Maybe it's time to make a change and reorient your church around this message. I'm going to assume you believe the gospel. I know you share it. But let's push that one step further. Is your church, in all its ministries, explicitly and intentionally centered on the gospel? If not, what's keeping you from repurposing your church through recentering on the gospel of Jesus?

Every church is driven by some purpose, whether it is clearly identified or not. Something is at the center of every church's ministry, the engine that runs everything. It is almost always a good thing that's located there—something true and biblical. But when you are driven by a purpose other than the gospel, the gospel ends up relegated to second place. The gospel becomes one more thing you do, perhaps mentioned in an invitation or an evangelism program.

This is a problem.

A gospel-driven church knows that the gospel isn't one feature of a church, one thing on the checklist, something useful in an evangelistic program. A gospel-driven church makes the gospel the unifying and motivating factor in everything they say and do.

- ▶ The gospel *makes* the church.
- ▶ The gospel makes the church one (with Christ and with each other).
- ▶ The gospel makes the church unique.
- ▶ The gospel makes the church powerful.
- ▶ The gospel makes the church holy.
- ▶ The gospel makes the church missional.

This good news isn't peripheral to your ministry. It's essential.

LifePoint Begins to Rethink the Formula

"I have this terrible suspicion that for twenty-two years I've been wasting my time."

Pastor Josh had taken Pastors Rob (growth) and Bob (care) out on the links. He was not having a good day.

"Well, every recreational golfer thinks that eventually," Bob joked.

Josh smiled. "I've probably been wasting my time here too. But I am up two strokes on you guys."

They'd just completed the fifth hole and were clambering back into the golf cart.

Rob said, "Nobody thinks you've wasted your time, Josh. Whatever is going on at LifePoint, and however you think we ought to adjust in response to it, there's absolutely no reason to be all 'doom and gloom' about it."

It had been three months since the survey results had come in. Josh and Felix presented the findings to the entire leadership team, giving a sense of the scope of the problem (as Josh saw it) and opening the floor to suggestions on how to address the issues. What he discovered was that, as Felix had helpfully pointed out, simply seeing the problem didn't give them the solution. And Josh suspected at least a couple of team members didn't think the problem was even a problem.

Since then, LifePoint had continued as it always had. Josh was in the middle of a teaching series on finances and had already preached messages on greed, debt, and work. The next Sunday, he would complete the series with a message on generosity. He and Matt, the creative arts director, had already sketched out the next teaching series, which would cover heroes of the Bible. But the whole thing had never been less exciting to him.

"I'm not trying to be doom and gloom," Josh said. "I'm sorry if it comes out that way. I wish I had the enthusiasm and energy Mike had when he was here. Or the even-keeled steadiness of Dave. Maybe I'm so weird and neurotic because they abandoned me," he joked. The other guys chuckled.

As they approached the next tee, Josh continued, "I can't shake this. I know trying to lead because of a weird feeling isn't leading at all. I have to figure out what the real issue is and what the real steps forward are. And I think we have to begin with the primary point of communication."

"The website?" Bob said.

"Ha. No, not the website. I mean the teaching. I've been doing it basically the same way from the very beginning. I've never questioned why I've never questioned it. I've gotten better at it, I think. But I've never questioned whether it was the right way to help people."

"You mean teaching in general?" Rob asked.

"No, I think there needs to be teaching," said Josh. "I just think that if twenty-two years of the same approach has not produced the results we always thought it was producing, maybe it's time to rethink the approach. Don't you think?"

Rob said, "I think it's worth asking the question, yes."

"Bob?" Josh asked.

Bob sort of shrugged. Doing things the same way he'd always done them was kind of Bob's thing. He didn't care what Josh preached or how Josh preached. Bob was a "go with the flow" kind of guy. But now the flow seemed to change direction, and he wasn't quite sure how he might fit into it. "If you think the teaching needs to change, Josh, then you know best. I personally think your teaching is great. Nobody's complaining about it. The church is full every Sunday, all four services. You have probably been able to guess that I don't see the situation the same way you and Rob and, I guess, Drake might see it, but I can support you and keep doing my thing."

Josh nodded. He wasn't surprised that Bob wasn't enthusiastic about change. At the moment, Josh wasn't either. But he could discern there may be some difficult conversations to be had in the weeks and months ahead.

He turned to Rob. "Let me ask you this. You're pastor for growth. How do people grow?"

"How do people grow?"

"Yeah. How do they change? I mean, yeah, the Holy Spirit. But what in your experience would sum up the experience that most transforms someone and helps them grow in their faith? For a new believer, old believer, in between believer."

Rob mulled it over. "I think I would say that I've seen the most faithfulness and consistency among people who have made a real connection with Jesus. They have a 'personal relationship.' I know that's a cliché, but the people I've seen who have stalled out, dropped out, or never really got started didn't really know Jesus. They liked Jesus. Or they liked some of the things he said. Or they were just interested in spirituality or faith in general. But over the last several years of doing discipleship and groups ministry, where I've seen the faith really 'click' for someone has to be when they've had some kind of encounter with Jesus."

Josh chewed on that as he teed up. Rob and Bob watched as he delivered a beautiful drive straight up the fairway. "I think I know what you mean," he said as Bob set up. "Think of your testimony. Or mine. Or almost anybody else's we know. I don't know anybody who legitimately fell in love with Jesus because someone told them to get their act together."

"Yeah," Rob said.

"Which is basically what I do every single week."

"What?"

"Tell people to get their act together. I mean, I'm nice about it. It's positive. It's inspirational. It's fun to listen to. At least, I hope it is. But when you boil it down, that's really all it is. Telling people what to do."

"You gotta tell people what to do," Bob said, as he waggled his driver between his stance. "The faith has to be lived."

Nobody said anything until Bob completed his drive. Then Rob said, "Bob, you're right. I don't think the answer is to stop helping people see that Christianity is practical. Of course it is. But maybe the emphasis on the practical stuff is not as effective in moving people to live practically." He seemed to think about his own words for a second, and added, "I know that sounds weird."

"It does," Josh said. "But I think it's right. I think my overemphasis on 'doing' has actually stifled growth. I'm not sure what my next step is, but I've been sensing for a while that my preaching is off. And I think if anything's going to change, it's that."

CHAPTER 5

Steering from the Stage

Changing the message changes the movement

"The world is a ship . . . and the pulpit is its prow."

So claims Herman Melville in his classic novel *Moby Dick*, and while Melville's claim may not exactly hold up in this post-Christian era of the West, it is certainly true for the local church. The preaching is the steering wheel of the church.

The pulpit is not the only place of leadership or influence. It may not even be the most frequent place of leadership or influence. But it is the most impactful place of leadership and influence. Everything that goes on in a local weekend gathering of a church—and the preaching and teaching specifically—directs the church's sense of identity, depth of belief, and quality of mission.

If a church is to be gospel-centered, it must have gospel-centered preaching. And if a church is to have gospel-centered preaching, it must have preaching that is substantially engaged with the Bible.

But this kind of preaching is not the norm for many attractional churches. Over twenty years ago when I began in ministry, I was trained in the seeker-church model. My instruction on preaching was not very robust, but I learned the basic pattern. We began by identifying a felt need in the congregation. What do people have trouble with? What are their concerns and struggles? Where do they need help or assistance or advice? It could be a relational issue or a personal issue or even a religious issue. But we always began with a felt need of some kind.

Then we thought carefully about the practical help we could give people in addressing that need. How can they overcome that challenge? What steps can be taken? What practices or habits can they develop to improve in those areas or achieve clarity or victory?

Once we had three to five action steps, we went looking for Bible verses to help support our points. You might use a concordance or a search program to find verses related to a particular topic or subject. Sometimes it was easy to find good verses, but sometimes it was difficult. If you could find a verse that used a word from your message point in the right way, it was like finding gold. A good sermon might have four or five Bible verses to support the various points of the message.

The problem with this approach ought to be obvious right away. First, it starts not with God's Word, but with our ideas about what people need. Then, after determining what people needed, we made God's Word serve our agenda rather than the other way around. The motivation behind this approach to preaching is sincere. The approach intends to reach lost people or spiritual seekers for God. The logic makes sense too. If we can show people that the Bible is relevant and applicable to their everyday lives, the reasoning goes, then they will be more likely to accept Christ.

But there are at least two errors embedded in this reasoning, no matter how sincere it might be. The first is mistaking *what the worship service is for*. The second is mistaking *what changes people*.

Who Is the Church For?

One of the reasons Christians have such diverse opinions about the elements in a worship service, from the service's style to its substance, is that many don't really know what the Bible teaches on the subject. Many of us assume that our gatherings can be any way we want them to be.[1]

But the Bible *does* provide guidance on what to do in our gatherings and who they are for. Look at one of the earliest church services, as seen in Acts 2:41–47:

So those who received his word were baptized, and there were added that day about three thousand souls. And they devoted themselves to the apostles' teaching and the fellowship, to the breaking of bread and the prayers. And awe came upon every soul, and many wonders and signs were being done through the apostles. And all who believed were together and had all things in common. And they were selling their possessions and belongings and distributing the proceeds to all, as any had need. And day by day, attending the temple together and breaking bread in their homes, they received their food with glad and generous hearts, praising God and having favor with all the people. And the Lord added to their number day by day those who were being saved.

This passage affirms, first of all, that the worship service existed almost exclusively for those who were already followers of Jesus.

Further, we note how the worship service is not really a program for individual Christians to get their weekly pick-me-up. Rather, it is a vital expression of the day-to-day "body life" enjoyed by the community of Christians in a given area. The big gathering was a more concentrated extension of their widespread "breaking [of] bread in their homes" (v. 46). The gospel is reconciling news. It unites individual sinners to God and through that union unites sinners to each other. "So those who received his word were baptized, and there were added that day about three thousand souls. And they devoted themselves to the apostles' teaching and the fellowship, to the breaking of bread and the prayers" (vv. 41–42). Note how the personal salvation of verse 41 transitions to the interpersonal relations of verse 42, and then note how this connection circles back to even more gospel reconciliation through gospel witness in verse 47.

This suggests that for the early church the weekend worship service was vitally connected to the experience of Christian fellowship, which is to say, the weekend worship service was not designed nor intended primarily as an evangelistic event for unbelievers.

I believe this is one of the fundamental flaws of the attractional church paradigm. The whole enterprise begins with a faulty assumption, a wrong idea of what the worship gathering *is* and what the church *is*.

In 1 Corinthians 14, Paul uses the word *outsider* (in vv. 16, 23–24) in reference to non-Christian visitors in the worship gathering. He says of course that our services should be clear to them in order to minimize the chance of confusion. He encourages hospitality and mindfulness about their presence in the service. But the very fact that he uses the word *outsider* should tell us that the unbeliever is not the primary audience of the weekend service.

Everyone who preaches should keep unbelievers in mind, addressing objections and questions that even skeptics might have to Christian truth claims. We ought to remember the preciousness of every unbelieving soul and seek to welcome them to the church service with grace and kindness. The Bible's teaching on corporate worship does not allow us to put unbelieving visitors out of sight and therefore out of mind. Nevertheless, the Bible's teaching on corporate worship also does not allow us to make unbelievers the focus of the service.

I know the seeker-focused approach to Sunday morning is widespread and influential, and I'm saying this is very unfortunate because it is also unbiblical.

The church is called to reach the lost, and we must be faithful. The church is called to be evangelistically hospitable and welcoming in its culture and evangelistically adaptable in its preaching and teaching (I'll say more on that in chapter 8). But the church's primary worship service should be designed with the saved in mind, not the seeker.

What Does the Church Need?

Even if I haven't convinced you yet, bear with me as I ask a couple of follow-up questions. If Christians are meant to be the primary participants of the worship service, what do Christians need to participate fully? If we assume that God designed the church for Christians, what about our gatherings might be helpful or necessary for Christian believers?

What believers need from their churches, above everything else and in every element experienced, is nourishment from the Word of God. This is what drives my concern and criticism of the attractional model, and it is, at least in part, what makes the reduction of Bible use in attractional services so unhelpful. Reducing reliance upon the Bible or removing it from a worship service in favor of practical help or biblically inspired principles is a sure sign that you don't know what a worship service is.

The church in Acts did not devote themselves to the apostles' teaching simply because they found it culturally relevant or more interesting than other teachings. If that were the case, we could easily choose another philosophy that is just as relevant or more interesting to our imaginations. Instead, the church in Acts devoted themselves to the teaching because they knew that nothing could be more important than *hearing from God.*

And the early church believed, as Jesus said, that the only way to live is to feed on God's Word (Matt. 4:4).

In 2008, *Christianity Today* reflected on the results from Willow's REVEAL survey, commenting on one of the "revealed" dysfunctions in the church's approach to discipleship: "The study shows that while Willow has been successfully meeting the spiritual needs of those who describe themselves as 'exploring Christianity' or "'growing in Christ,' it has been less successful at doing so with those who self-report as being 'close to Christ' or 'Christ-centered.'"

Is it enough simply to get sheep in the pasture while leaving them thereafter unfed?

This occurs by design in the attractional church. I was once involved in a lively exchange on Twitter with an attractional church apologist, and he was making the case that we should treat the worship gathering like an evangelistic conversation with the lost. His case began, "Imagine you are in a coffee shop with an unbeliever." I responded (basically), "I don't have to imagine that. I've been in that coffee shop and other places like it numerous times." My point was that you don't have to treat the worship service like a coffee shop conversation if you're actually engaged in coffee shop conversations with unbelievers. Eventually we both agreed that evangelistic conversations in coffee shops (or elsewhere) don't need to sound like sermons. The point where we diverged was whether the gathering of the saints for worship should be reduced to a coffee shop conversation with a lost person. I argued that this is a fundamental misunderstanding of what the worship service is. This misunderstanding only breeds more errant practices, like the habit of conducting worship gatherings without any reference to the Bible, as if our very existence does not center on the power and authority of the Word of God.

People on all sides of this debate will agree that *the message moves people*. The pulpit is the prow of the church. Where it goes, the church will go.

Do we want the church to move in a direction that emphasizes that the church exists to meet their needs (consumerism)? Or do we want the church to understand the Bible as the central, most authoritative, most life-giving well of revelation available to them?

What Is Gospel-Driven Preaching?

The great Welsh preacher Dr. Martyn Lloyd-Jones once said,

> I have often discouraged the taking of notes while I am preaching. . . . The first and primary object of preaching is not only to give information. It is, as Edwards says, to produce an impression. It is the impression at the time that matters, even more than what you can remember subsequently. . . . While you are writing your notes, you may be missing something of the impact of the Spirit.[2]

This is a fundamentally different way of thinking about preaching than we tend to find in the attractional church. But some pastors make a mistake here. A pastor may seek to preach to produce an impression, but he thinks this means changing the style of his preaching.

The antidote for preaching that is moralistic ("do these things; don't do these other things") or pragmatic ("if you do these things, you will get these other things") isn't to adopt a verse-by-verse or expositional approach. Expositional preaching (carefully unpacking the meaning of a particular text of Scripture) is the place to start, if only because it demonstrates that our sermon is serving God's Word rather than the other way around. But it's not enough. It's entirely possible to preach a moralistic and pragmatic sermon using the expositional method.

What Lloyd-Jones is getting at is not a style, and it is only superficially a method. It is a conviction, a reliance, and a substantive message that connects the biblical text being preached to the metanarratives of God's kingdom, God's glory, and God's saving work through Christ. Gospel-driven preaching is preaching that proclaims and exults in the revealing of God's glory in Christ.[3] We see this reflected in the Scriptures and throughout church history whenever the gospel was treasured. Gospel-driven preaching involves drawing out the meaning and applying it in a way that points people toward a response like the response formed in us by the gospel. Though it is an Old Testament reference, Nehemiah 8:1–12 remains a helpful example not only of expositional preaching (Ezra and the scribes read from the Scriptures) but of the pastoral application to the people (they "gave the sense, so that the people understood the reading" [v. 8]).

Let's take my definition step by step and examine each component.

Gospel-Driven Preaching Proclaims

Sadly, proclamation seems to have gone the way of the dodo in many churches.

What has replaced it could be called teaching, but in some cases, it's closer to a pep talk. The role of the preacher has been replaced by a life coach or a public therapist. We replaced the pulpit with a coffee stand and an open Bible with an LED screen and turned the preacher into a presenter and the sermon into a TED talk.

None of that critique is to suggest that preaching should be dry, academic, or stuffy. But the evangelical preaching flavor of the month tends to emphasize informal chit-chat over authoritative declaration.

It's okay to be creative in preaching, and it's certainly okay to be excellent and winsome, but the preacher of God's Word must remember that at the end of the day, it is not creativity or excellence or winsomeness that wins hearts to Christ but the sufficient and powerful Word of God. The gravity, the weight, the importance, and the authority of the Bible is what people need. They do not need our advice; they need an announcement, a word from the One who made them.

Gospel-Driven Preaching Exults

Good Christian preaching unleashes joy. The preaching of a sermon, then, is not simply to fuel worship of God but is itself—in the very act—worship of God too.

We live in a day when "worship" is equated primarily with music. Sometimes when the singing stops, we say things like, "Now that we've worshiped, we will hear from God's Word." Or sometimes we refer to the singing as a "time of worship." But the whole gathering is meant to be a time of worship! Preaching and listening to preaching is no less worship than singing. Or at least, it shouldn't be.

As I said earlier, the aim in preaching is not to show off what you can do or to impress people with your ability or dazzle them with your creativity. The point is to point them to the living God in the content and through your passion so that they might respond to God's good news in worship.

Notice Ezra's demeanor during his great proclamation, recorded in the book of Nehemiah: "And Ezra blessed the LORD, the great God, and all the people answered, 'Amen, Amen,' lifting up their hands. And they bowed their heads and worshiped the LORD with their faces to the ground" (8:6). The people are worshiping in response to the Word preached. Preaching that exults in the exalting of God requires a preacher whose affections have been affected by God's Word. You cannot give what you don't have. And you can't model what you don't know.

The church desperately needs more preachers who exult.

Gospel-Driven Preaching Reveals the Glory of God in Christ

Imagine preaching a sermon verse by verse through a passage of Scripture. It could be an Old Testament text or a New Testament text, perhaps something from one of Paul's Epistles. Now imagine you get to the end of the message without mentioning Jesus. Could you rightly say you preached a Christian message?

Some preachers assume the answer is yes, especially if they are a Christian preaching in a Christian church. But every week Jehovah's Witnesses, Mormons, and Unitarians hear messages from the Bible that do not include the gospel. What makes a lesson from the Bible on kindness or holiness that doesn't mention the gospel of Jesus anymore Christian than the same kind of sermon preached in any one of those non-Christian places of worship?

A New Testament sermon can be preached in an unchristian way.

So when I say that Christian preaching "gives the sense" of the text, "the sense" of any given Bible passage includes the gospel message. To make sense of any passage of Scripture, we have to see what it means to its original hearers, but we also need to understand what it means in the light of Scripture as a whole. How does it fit into the grand storyline of Christ the entire Bible is telling? Remember that on the road to Emmaus Jesus told his disciples that even the whole Old Testament was ultimately about him (Luke 24:27).

Therefore, every sermon has to do some serious work in showing the glory of Christ from whatever text the preacher is preaching. Christ's glory changes people (2 Cor. 3:18), so we must emphasize his glory over our good ideas.

The primary way we reveal God's glory in Christ is by saturating our preaching in the gospel of grace. We have all sinned and fallen short of the glory of God (Rom. 3:23). If our sermons present people with the law alone or give them a list of to-dos or advice to follow, we will only exacerbate their sense of alienation when they fail to do everything we've told them to do to experience success as a Christian.

We are starving for the glory of God. We die without it. Every week people come into church services parched, thirsty, and starving.

When we preach sermons that are mostly law, it's like giving them a jug of sand to drink. Gospel-driven preaching is proclamation that exults in exposing God's glory, and we behold this glory in the announcement of the gospel of Jesus Christ, who according to Hebrews 1 is the radiance of the glory of God.

Again: sermons that have nothing of the gospel of Jesus Christ in them are *not Christian sermons*. A Christian may be preaching them. The text may be a Christian text. But if the gospel isn't there, neither is real Christianity.

I'm reminded of this stirring and humorous story told by Charles Spurgeon:

A young man had been preaching in the presence of a venerable divine, and after he had done he went to the old minister, and said, "What do you think of my sermon?"

"A very poor sermon, indeed," said he.

"A poor sermon?" said the young man, "it took me a long time to study it."

"Ay, no doubt of it."

"Why, did you not think my explanation of the text a very good one?"

"Oh, yes," said the old preacher, "very good, indeed."

"Well, then, why do you say it is a poor sermon? Didn't you think the metaphors were appropriate, and the arguments conclusive?"

"Yes, they were very good as far as that goes, but still it was a very poor sermon."

"Will you tell me why you think it a poor sermon?"

"Because," said he, "there was no Christ in it."

"Well," said the young man, "Christ was not in the text; we are not to be preaching Christ always, we must preach what is in the text."

So the old man said, "Don't you know, young man, that from every town, and every village, and every little hamlet in England, wherever it may be, there is a road to London?"

"Yes," said the young man.

"Ah!" said the old divine "and so from every text in Scripture, there is a road to the metropolis of the Scriptures, that is Christ. And, my dear brother, your business is, when you get to a text, to say, 'Now what is the road to Christ?' and then preach a sermon, running along the road towards the great metropolis—Christ. And," said he, "I have never yet found a text that had not got a road to Christ in it, and if I ever do find one that has not got a road to Christ in it, I will make one; I will go over hedge and ditch but I would get at my Master, for the sermon cannot do any good unless there is a savor of Christ in it."[4]

A "savor" of Christ—that's what our hearts are starving for.

We can taste the goodness of the gospel even in our Old Testament preaching passage:

> And Nehemiah, who was the governor, and Ezra the priest and scribe, and the Levites who taught the people said to all the people, "This day is holy to the LORD your God; do not mourn or weep." For all the people wept as they heard the words of the Law. Then he said to them, "Go your way. Eat the fat and drink sweet wine and send portions to anyone who has nothing ready, for this day is holy to our Lord. And do not be grieved, for the joy of the LORD is your strength." So the Levites calmed all the people, saying, "Be quiet, for this day is holy; do not be grieved." And all the people went their way to eat and drink and to send portions and to make great rejoicing, because they had understood the words that were declared to them. (Neh. 8:9–12)

Notice how the law did its job. It instructs. It reveals sinfulness. So what do the ministers do? They don't want people to leave heartbroken!

If people leave your church every week feeling crushed, with one more thing they need to do to please God, something is wrong. Pastor, if you're constantly giving out ten steps or tips or how-tos, you're crushing people.

I know making this shift can be difficult. Many of us were not trained or mentored to preach this way. Many of us struggle to find Christ in every text we study. It feels new and unnatural to many of us. But until we begin working to discover the glory of Christ in each passage of Scripture, we will fail to adequately preach what people actually need. They can get advice from daytime television. They can get fear and browbeating from internet news. They can get inspirational fortunes from the self-help shelves at the local bookstore. The only place they will receive the transforming glory of Christ is in the Spirit-inspired Word of God.

So work hard. Read the right commentaries, consult the right teachers, listen to the right leaders—the ones that help you see Jesus in the Bible. Don't simply come to the Bible thinking about how to leverage it to what you want to say. Savor its goodness. Stare at it until the beauty of Christ begins to poke through the shadows of law. And don't be afraid to embrace the uniqueness of preaching Christ as the point of the whole Bible.

If preaching God's Word awakens in others a deeper longing for Christ, you've done more than what a hundred practical tips can accomplish. When a sinner encounters glory in the gospel, and it is spiritually applied to their hearts, they will be changed forever.

Preaching Is the First Change to Effect Change

"Hearing a sermon is not like hearing a lecture," Ray Ortlund says. "It is your meeting with the living Christ. It is you seeing his glory, so that you can feel it and be changed by it."[5] I hope that this book is becoming more "practical" as it progresses. When we talk about being gospel-centered, we are not talking about becoming impractical. There are things you *do* to be gospel-centered. What we need to avoid is a pragmatic philosophy that drives our ministry. So what's a practical step you can make here? Aside from the preliminary work of research and an assessment of the congregation, the first and quickest thing you can change in your church is the preaching.

The further your preaching methods are from gospel-driven preaching, the more jarring a change may be for your congregation. If you have only recently made this transition, it's unlikely that you have entirely figured out how to shift gears just yet. Move slowly. Incrementally figure it out while your congregation incrementally adjusts.

Preaching is a good place to begin. The one thing the preaching pastor can control is what and how he preaches on Sunday morning. So stretch yourself. Check out some of the resources for preaching listed at the back of this book. Listen to the sermon podcasts of preachers who exemplify gospel-centered preaching like John Piper, Matt Chandler, Tim Keller, D. A. Carson, and Mark Dever. These men preach with different styles, different personalities, and in different contexts. This showcases that gospel-centered preaching isn't defined by any of these things. It's a posture and an approach, a way of approaching the Word that highlights the glory of Christ.

Of course, your preaching needs to be your own. The message needs to be in your voice. But as you pursue repurposing your preaching around God's power to change us in Christ, you can find inspiration and influence from the example of others. There are many gospel applications you can make in any given sermon. Here are some common approaches to texts that don't explicitly mention Jesus (as we find in much of the Old Testament):

- ▶ Show how your Old Testament passage prophesies about or otherwise foreshadows Christ or some aspect of his saving work.
- ▶ Show how your Old Testament "hero" was a "type" of Christ, preparing us for Jesus's perfect courage, mercy, faith.
- ▶ Show how a passage presents a problem for which Jesus is the ultimate solution.
- ▶ Connect the practical applications and imperatives to gospel declarations and indicatives, showing how "doing" flows from "being."

▶ Show how a narrative passage fits into the big story of the Bible, the story of God's grace given in Christ.

There are many more ways to do this, and of course it is easier to make the connection if the passage explicitly articulates or points to the gospel message. But these suggestions may give you a good start on changing the way you look at a text in your sermon prep.

Since preaching changes people, hearers will learn, over time, how to make these applications in their personal devotional times and service to the world. Imagine what might happen if people were equipped to see how the gospel speaks to their struggles, fears, and doubts, as well as their sins. Gospel-driven preaching becomes substantially more difficult if you doubt that it's something you *must* do, not just something you *can* do. If you know you must, figuring out how to implement it will follow in due time.

Do you want to change the direction of your church? Change the orientation of your preaching from lifeless law to the power of grace. Changing the message will change the movement.

LifePoint's First Gridlock

Josh and Matt had been sitting in the conference for two hours, noodling around in sketchbooks, alternating between long periods of silent thinking and bursts of creative exchange. Something wasn't—to use Matt's word—*flowing*.

The truth was, Josh was between visions. He knew the long-standing and most-definable vision for the church was no longer viable. But he hadn't quite figured out what the next one was. More conversations with Rob after the golf outing helped. Reading some books helped. Listening to some podcasts helped. But Josh knew the vision for a more—what? a more "gospelly" church?—couldn't be borrowed. It had to be owned. Because he didn't quite grasp it himself, he was struggling to pass it on to others. While he and Matt were usually done with their series brainstorming meetings in two hours, they found themselves stuck. Two hours in, it was as if they hadn't started.

"I just don't know what you want," Matt said.

"Yeah, I know. That's on me. All I really know is what I don't want."

"I mean, these songs are good songs. Our people really respond well to them."

"I know, I know. But they don't fit where I want to go."

"Well, you're teaching on Joseph, yeah? Daniel. David. And Samson."

"Right."

"There aren't any songs about those guys."

Josh laughed. "I know. That's not what I'm asking for."

Matt smiled, "Okay. Just making sure. I'm just going off the themes you mentioned before."

Josh said, "Yeah, that's where I'm stuck. Because the themes are fine, but it's just the same thing I've always done."

"Well, you know, man," Matt said, "what we've always done *works.*"

Josh thought, *No, it doesn't. Not in the way we need it to.*

"What I mean is," Matt said, "you tell me the David message is on courage, I got songs. You tell me Daniel is on faith, I got songs. Joseph is on forgiveness . . . well, I kinda have some songs on that." He paused, smiled. "Maybe."

Josh leaned back in his chair. A thought struck him. Maybe the reason he and Matt were having so many problems with this process was that the process was all wrong. He was trying to superimpose gospel content into a system that had not been informed by the gospel.

What if the gospel doesn't just affect the content you communicate on Sunday mornings but even the very way you communicate it? What if the gospel is meant to impact the system, the presuppositions, the whole thing?

"Let's start over," Josh said. "Tell me this: What's the music *for?*"

CHAPTER 6

Building Your Service around Beholding

Designing the gathering for real transformation

"The whole creative package," Matt said, "is meant to set the mood for meeting God and also for the message."

"Set the mood?"

Josh was repeating the phrase like it confused him, but he wasn't confused at all. He knew exactly why they conducted worship the way they had been for years. It was one of LifePoint's most compelling features—vibrant, relevant "worship experiences." Matt was incredibly good not just at music but in helping his creative team execute stage sets, lighting design, and video elements that drew people in and, yes, set a mood.

Josh was repeating the phrase mainly because it suddenly sounded... *off.* It sounded as off as his preaching.

He knew that Matt was probably nervous, though Matt didn't show it. If anything, he looked perturbed. Really, he just looked lethargic. For a creative guy, devoted to innovation, thinking outside the box, pushing the boundaries, and freedom of expression, he really didn't like having to do something new.

But Josh knew why. It wasn't a character flaw, not really. Matt was a good guy who loved Jesus and loved people. But he'd also grown up in a restrictive Christian environment. The church he grew up in was very rigid, practically fundamentalist. The preaching was loud but boring. The people were sweet but devoted to ritual. The music always sounded like a formality, like the congregation knew they had to sing in church so they might as well.

Forget anything creative or expressive. As a free-thinking kid with a bit of wildness mixed with creative gifts, Matt could very easily have ended up outside the church altogether. Many young people like him leave entirely. But he did believe. He was grateful for the faith he'd gotten from his upbringing, but he was happy to find a succession of churches that not only embraced creative thinking like his but also employed it. He felt useful to the kingdom for the first time in college, when he began leading worship. As he learned more and became more skilled, his gifts became more and more in demand at youth and college events.

Eventually he was hired (by Josh) to help LifePoint do exactly what he said they were doing: set the mood. But now he might be feeling a little panicky, like the rug was about to get pulled out from under him.

Matt said, "The music prepares people for the teaching, of course, but it also helps them feel connected to God."

"Okay," Josh said. "I think I agree with that. I think I'm pulling away from the 'helping them feel stuff' stuff, but I do agree that the music should help people connect to God. I just wonder if we could be more verbal about that."

"Like a spoken word type thing?"

"Heh-heh. No. Well . . . maybe. No, what I mean is, we should probably sing songs that have more direct content on the teaching themes. Rather than creating a mood, actually communicating truths. To reinforce them somehow or help people rehearse them."

"You're talking about an entire new catalog of songs, probably."

"Is that bad?"

Matt mulled it over. "I don't think so. But we're talking about resetting everything. Retraining our vocalists and musicians. Right now, we make time for a couple of new songs every six months or so. A reboot would be really disruptive."

"I know. I think it could be worth it. You don't need to throw everything out and start with all new songs. Maybe we can sort through some of the songs together, or you and Drake could get together, since I know some of your team members lead at the student events too. We could introduce new songs gradually."

"Yeah, I think if we just worked up to it, we could manage it better. And probably wouldn't freak too many people out." (Josh knew Matt was referring mostly to himself.)

"Thanks, man. Why don't we take a break for now? Email me the top ten songs we have in the rotation right now, include the lyrics, and I will look them over. We can probably keep some. And I will do some research on some other songs that we might begin to pepper in. We won't change much anytime soon. But I do want to be moving forward on this."

"Sure, okay," Matt said.

"Also, one more thing. I wonder if we could talk about maybe turning the lights up a bit and turning the sound down a bit."

Matt blinked. "Okay." He looked like he'd just been given a year to live.

McWorship: Billions Served

Do you remember the Trojan rabbit scene in the movie *Monty Python and the Holy Grail*? If you haven't seen the movie, King Arthur and his idiot knights decide to invade a French castle in their own version of the mythological Trojan horse. They build a gigantic wooden rabbit, hide themselves inside it, and "gift" themselves to the French, whom they hope will bring them inside the castle walls, at which point the knights can pour out after dark and launch their surprise attack.

The knights watch the French bring the rabbit into the castle with mirthful glee. Until they realize they never got inside the rabbit.

A lot of attractional worship services are like that plan of attack. At its inception, the attractional church was about getting as many people as possible inside the doors so they could hear the good news of Jesus Christ. In my youth ministry days, we used all manner of traditionally adolescent enticements to do this—junk food, crazy games, loud music. The "big church" services utilized the attractional paradigm to create grown-up versions of these enticements, ostensibly to contextualize the message. A cynical person might call this approach to ministry "the ol' bait and switch." Get 'em inside with some cool stuff and then share the gospel with your captive audience.

But over the years something unfortunate happened. The dictum that what you win people with is what you win them *to* increasingly proved to be true. The gospel of Christ's finished work was gradually relegated to the end of the service, an addendum to the contextualized, application-focused messages and relevant worship experiences. The gospel was gradually pushed to the end of an entire message series, until it became something you saved for special occasions. Today, in many churches, it has been replaced altogether by the shiny legalism of moralistic therapeutic deism.

Over time, the attractional church model became all bait and no switch. It's like the Trojan rabbit of Monty Python's Arthurian nincompoops—we've smuggled it inside the castle (church) walls with nothing inside.

When the mood is the point, the message becomes expendable.

As a result, many who have spent decades inside the system can't distinguish between attractive and attractional, practical and pragmatic. When we lose the centrality of the gospel, we lose the ability to discern and think biblically about worship. The "experience" of worship has become an end unto itself. In many churches, the experience of worship is the true object of worship. Worship has become a consumer good, a commodity, with churches trying to outperform, outproduce, and outpassion *other churches*. This self-interested approach to music is a fitting complement to the self-help messages taught in such churches. Even if there is a lot of God-talk going on, the true object of worship—the one the product aims to serve—is the worshiper. But this is problematic. As scholar N. T. Wright says, "To enjoy worship for its own sake, or simply out of a cultural appreciation of the 'performance' . . . would be like Moses coming upon a burning bush and deciding to cook his lunch on it."[1]

How do we know if we've crossed the line? The mood becomes the point when the worshiper's feelings become the primary object of the worship service. And this is widespread today. We produce it, package it, and promote it in nearly every corner of evangelicalism. You can practically franchise it. In many worship services today, you cannot find a local embodied expression of the biblical message. Instead, you find a replication or appropriation of whatever is popular in the broader culture. A Big Mac tastes the same in Kansas City, Missouri, as it does in Sydney, Australia—I've had one both places. The same is true in any two randomly selected attractional churches—the worship product looks the same. Call it McWorship. Business is good, and the customer is king.

As with our approach to worship in preaching, our understanding of worship in song (and other creative elements) is largely dependent upon our presuppositions about the church itself. Who is the church for? What should the service do?

Unbiblical answers to these questions lead us to build our services in disordered ways.

Is Your Worship Service Upside Down?

As we discussed in the last chapter, our church worship gatherings ought to be welcoming and comprehensible to unbelievers, but the Bible does not envision orienting the gathering to them. There is no biblical precedent for the seeker-targeted service, and it's not even the most effective way for your church to reach lost people. If your church orients its weekend gathering around "reaching seekers," it's quite possible you have adopted some of the working assumptions I'll outline in the following section. These programmatic arrangements turn the biblical shape of evangelism and mission upside down.

Emphasizing Feelings before and Instead of Doctrine

Many churches describe their gatherings as "experiences." I want to gently suggest that this is an incorrect way of thinking about what happens on Sunday mornings. Many people may experience God there, but you cannot create an experience of God. The worship gathering ought to seek to orchestrate an encounter with God, not an *experience* of him.

Is it really so wrong to try to "create an experience"? What's wrong with that? Disney does it. Chain restaurants do it. Shopping malls do it. Why not churches?

Economist James Gilmore, author of *The Experience Economy*, is an expert on "creating experiences." He cautions against replicating such experiences in worship services. As recorded in Skye Jethani's book *The Divine Commodity*, Gilmore's conversation with *Leadership Journal* staffers Marshall Shelley (MS), Eric Reed (ER), and Kevin Miller (KM) explains why. This is such an important exchange, that I quoted it in my previous book *The Prodigal Church* as well:

> MS: So how does all this "experience providing" apply to the church?
>
> Gilmore: It doesn't. When the church gets into the business of staging experiences, that quickly becomes idolatry.
>
> MS: I'm stunned. So, you don't encourage churches to use your elements of marketable experiences to create attractive experiences for their attenders?
>
> Gilmore: No. The organized church should never try to stage a God experience.
>
> KM: When people come to church, don't they expect an experience of some kind? Consumers approach the worship service with the same mindset as they do a purchase.
>
> Gilmore: Increasingly, you find people talking about the worship experience rather than the worship service. That reflects what's happening in the outside world. I'm dismayed to see churches abandon the means of grace that God ordains simply to conform to the patterns of the world.
>
> KM: So, what happens in church? Are people getting a service, because they're helped to do something they couldn't do

on their own, that is, get closer to God? Or are they getting an experience, the encounter with God through worship?

Gilmore: The word "getting" is, I think, the problem with contemporary Christianity. God is the audience of worship. What you get is, quite frankly, irrelevant as a starting point.

ER: But people, especially unchurched people, don't perceive it that way. They're expecting some return.

Gilmore: They come that way at first: "Give me, feed me, make me feel good." But they should be led to say, "Hey, this is not about me, God. Worship is to glorify you."

KM: But if my mission is to reach a consumerist culture—if I'm going to get a hearing for my message—then I'm going to have to provide something that the consumer considers of value.

Gilmore: That is the argument. But the only thing of value the church has to offer is the gospel. I believe that one result of the emerging Experience Economy will be a longing for authenticity. To the extent that the church stages worldly experiences, it will lose its effectiveness.[2]

Don't miss that statement by James Gilmore: "The only thing of value the church has to offer is the gospel."

I know, I know. Many of us come from traditional church backgrounds where doctrine was all that mattered and the people were cold or harsh or uncaring about their neighbors. That's another way to be upside down and antigospel. In many evangelical communities today, we see a downplaying of theology and doctrinal truth in order to make way for personal feelings and individual preferences. The problems with this approach are numerous, but the two main problems I'd cite are these:

- ▸ Feelings about God detached from knowledge of God indicates we are more worshipers of feelings—of ourselves.
- ▸ Just as serious, perhaps, is expecting lost people to sing songs about their feelings about a God they don't believe in.

Too much of our Sunday morning worship sets the cart of affections before the horse of belief.

At the risk of wearying repetition, I want to clarify that emotions are not bad or wrong. In fact, how we feel and express our emotions is often a key indicator of our heart's desires. As Pastor Bob Kauflin writes,

> The problem is *emotionalism*, not *emotions*. Emotionalism pursues feelings as an end in themselves. It's wanting to feel something with no regard for how that feeling is produced or its ultimate purpose. Emotionalism can also view heightened emotions as the infallible sign that God is present.[3]

The problem of emotionalism is often related to the persistent problem of singing theologically shallow or doctrinally vacant songs. When our emotions are aligned with biblical truth and accurate knowledge of God and the gospel, the result is genuine worship, worship in Spirit and truth. But the attractional model gets the cart before the horse. It attempts to get folks singing songs about a God they don't (yet) believe in or know. It introduces feelings and experiences prior to biblical knowledge and truth, and this leads to feelings that are wrongheaded. Putting feelings before doctrine promotes upside-down worship.

Lost People Are Given Religious Homework

When the attractional church orients worship around the lost and offers a steady diet of inspirational advice, or biblically based application points, it forgets that the practical side of Christianity is aimed solely at *Christians*. The expectation of being able to obey and please God is only placed on those who have both a heart changed to desire obedience and the Spiritual power to carry it out.

All the law can do to the heart of a lost person is crush it. The law brings truth about our sinfulness and inability to please God, but it does not help us pay our debt (Rom. 3:20, 28). If anything, the law increases our debt (Rom. 5:20). This "crushing" is a necessary work because it prepares people to relish the goodness of grace. But until that heart is captured by grace, the law will be a burden, not a delight. Trying to do good things without the goodness of Christ is simply self-righteousness.

In seeker-oriented worship, we direct a steady diet of "how to" at people who have yet to receive a heart full of *"want* to." Unbelievers should hear the commands and applications of God's designs, to be sure, but the primary power this application of the law has on the heart of a "seeker" is one of conviction, not empowerment. The commands of the Bible—whether they are of the "don't commit adultery" variety (negative law) or the "love your neighbor" variety (positive law)—have no power to help us in themselves. They only tell us what to do, or not to do. *They can't help us do it.*

According to the Bible, only one thing has power: the gospel of Jesus Christ. In Ephesians 3:7, Paul says the gospel was given to him by God's power. In 1 Thessalonians 1:5, he says the gospel is accompanied with power. In 1 Corinthians 1:18, he says the message of the gospel is the power of God. In Romans 1:16 he writes, "For I am not ashamed of the gospel, for it is the power of God for salvation to everyone who believes, to the Jew first and also to the Greek." In 2 Corinthians 3:18, he says real change comes from beholding the glory of Jesus in the gospel, and the context of that chapter lays out his teaching on the gospel's superiority to the law. And in Titus 2:11–12, he says that it is grace, not law, that trains us to live holy lives.

The power for salvation and the sanctification that follows comes only from the gospel, not the law. In other words, the power for to-dos comes not from to-dos, but from the "was-done" of Jesus Christ.

Knowing this, isn't it a little strange to emphasize to lost people a list of things to do rather than emphasizing what's been *done*? If your weekend teaching is heavy on how-tos for the lost, you're giving religious homework to people who don't have the right heart to receive it, who will experience it as self-righteousness. This is philosophically backward and theologically upside down.

Gospel Invitations Are Offered after a Legal Message

Let's consider what happens at a worship service in a typical attractional church. The pastor spends thirty to forty-five minutes encouraging a lost person to do a bunch of things that please God, and afterward, he adds an invitation to receive Jesus. We can refer to this service order as a "law message with a gospel postscript," and I believe it creates spiritual whiplash. What do I mean?

When the majority of a message communicates things someone can do that please God (law) and then quickly pivots to an invitation to believe a truth the teacher hasn't spent much time communicating, it is confusing at best, spiritually dangerous at worst. For one, it creates the impression that the gospel postscript is unnecessary or optional. Even worse, it's unbiblical, because the Bible repeatedly teaches that the kind of obedience to God that pleases God comes *after* our heart has been changed by grace. Religious behavior modification doesn't glorify God; it glorifies self. If we preach a sermon filled with tips for behavior modification and then invite people to receive grace, it is disjointed, and it leads to a strange "gospel." We've suddenly changed subjects, and people aren't always sure how the two are connected. Going in one direction (law) and suddenly being jolted in another (grace) can distort people's understanding of the Bible, diminish their view of the gospel's glory, and disrupt their sense of security in Christ—it causes spiritual whiplash.

I remember hearing a well-known attractional pastor preach a sermon for women in which he repeated, over and over again, that God finds them captivating. The entire message was about how knocked out, bowled over, and weak-kneed God was about women. Then at the end, in his invitation to receive Jesus, the pastor said God would cover their ugliness and shame. The contrast was strange. The promise to cover ugliness felt tacked-on to the sermon. It is one thing to be loved *because* you are beautiful, and it's another to be ugly and loved despite that, because God's love *makes* you beautiful.

This is an extreme example, but I think it is a fitting one, given how much evangelical preaching is a spiritualized version of Stuart

Smalley's affirmation, "You're good enough, smart enough, and, doggone it, people like you." The predominant message today teaches self-worth by means of positive affirmation, telling people they're beautiful, unique snowflakes with limitless potential. How do you preach this and then segue into the utter emptiness and need we have apart from God? "Wait a minute," we think. "You just went on and on about how awesome I am. Now you say I'm not?"

It's upside down.

We must return to the biblical order here, treating the practicality of the Christian life as the application of the message, *not the message itself*. Reordering our understanding of law and gospel also helps us understand the point of the worship gathering itself, including how best to utilize the music and song. The worship service is primarily about helping people behold and believe, not behave and feel. Our behavior and feelings are implications of our beholding and believing, but the beholding and believing must come first. Remember, you are designing an encounter, not an experience.

So how do you do that?

The Four Irreducible Elements of Gospel-Driven Worship

Biblically speaking, the corporate gathering of believers in Christ should consist of four primary elements: preaching, praying, singing, and eating. We enjoy the liberty of including other elements in our gatherings, especially things we see occurring in the Bible, but without these four primary elements, worship gatherings would be incomplete.

Preaching

Since we discussed preaching in the previous chapter, I won't repeat myself too much. I will, however, reiterate that the preaching event is the centerpiece of the worship gathering because it is where we most declaratively and authoritatively hear from God. God speaking to us is always more important than us speaking to him, although both lanes of communication must be open for us to grow as Christians.

It's important to think of the sermon both as an act of worship and as a *call* to worship. When I critique some forms of invitations or altar calls, I'm not saying the sermon should not invite people to repent and believe. The gospel is not fully preached until people have been called to respond. The call can sometimes look like practical application points, but more generally it looks like prophetic pleading that urges hearers to turn from their way and embrace the way of Jesus.

It's also important to preach doctrine and theology. If Jonathan Edwards is correct when he tells us that a growing interest in theology is a mark of a genuine move of the Holy Spirit, then we should be serving our people these glorious truths. If you think doctrine is dry, perhaps you've only heard it from dry preachers. Doctrine cannot be divorced from devotion or the Word divorced from worship. True worship must have the right object, and having the right object requires knowing the object. And the object of worship is God. As N. T. Wright states,

> If your idea of God, if your idea of the salvation offered in Christ, is vague or remote, your idea of worship will be fuzzy and ill-formed. The closer you get to the truth, the clearer becomes the beauty, and the more you will find worship welling up within you. That's why theology and worship belong together. The one isn't just a head-trip; the other isn't just emotion.[4]

Praying

I emphasized the need for prayer earlier, so let me reiterate that the experience of the supernaturality of Christianity is impotent without the submission of Christians to God in prayer. Every significant revival in church history was precipitated by both the faithful preaching of the gospel word and the fervent, frequent prayers of the people. The reason prayer doesn't find its way into our worship services is because we are too busy trying to manipulate God rather than supplicating before him. We have traded in the human weakness required for prayer, in which we explicitly and implicitly confess that we serve and need God, for a worship experience trying to summon God and charge him with making us feel a certain way.

Worship services that do not include much prayer, or have perfunctory prayers that function as transitions, run the risk of representing God through the lens of the prosperity gospel, as if we are in charge, calling God to account.

The early church devoted themselves to prayer in their gatherings (Acts 2:42), and Paul instructs the church to include prayer in their services in 1 Timothy 2:1 and gives lengthy instructions on corporate prayer in 1 Corinthians 11 and 14.

Why all this emphasis on prayer?

Because prayer is an expression of dependence on God. The less we pray, the more we think we're doing fine without him. We can even end up doing religious and spiritual things without relying on him. It's not enough to do the right things; we must do the right things *in the Lord's power*. Prayer helps us tap into that.

Singing

"Let the word of Christ dwell in you richly," Paul says, "teaching and admonishing one another in all wisdom, singing psalms and hymns and spiritual songs, with thankfulness in your hearts to God" (Col. 3:16). Are we free to sing anything we wish? Is it okay to open a worship service with a song from pop radio? Do the songs set the mood and create a vibe?

Earlier I mentioned that the primary problem with the attractional approach to music and singing is that it is feelings-based and not faith-fueling. But a related problem is that it is undeniably individualistic. One thing the attractional paradigm does extremely well is create environments where masses of people can gather to have an individual worship experience. In many attractional worship sets, people can't hear each other. Often, they can't hear themselves. But is this the "vibe" Paul intends Christians to experience when he writes about worship in Colossians 3:16?

Pastor Matt Capps writes:

When the church as a whole sings, there is "speaking one to another" that admonishes and encourages us corporately in the faith. In this sense, we might even say the loudest sound in a room should be the congregation. In Christ, we are one body. Demonstrating that reality in worship requires that we actually be able to hear ourselves, and hear one another singing alongside us. It is a corporate affirmation that says we are one, and we believe what we are singing regardless of where we are spiritually or emotionally as individuals!

This is why our church family leans heavily towards congregational singing. Americans and Westerners are accustomed to professional-quality and performance-oriented music. And so many worship services are dimly lit, with the band cranked up so loud that you can't even hear yourself sing, much less those around you. In these atmospheres, I have often heard the worship leader lament, "Why isn't anyone singing?" Because the form of a congregation's worship undoubtedly affects the congregation's participation in worship. In performance-oriented services, the congregation becomes utterly passive. This leaves the church longing. Deep in our souls, we long to sing together. The church body is made for corporate worship. Let us not only allow, but lead the church to sing to God, but also to sing for one another.[5]

Lyrics are another crucially important element. Many songs employed by attractional churches highlight feelings, impressions, and visions. There is nothing wrong with using such language, if sparingly. The Bible is a beautiful book full of rich expressions, metaphors, and images. But the Bible also features propositional truth, and this propositional truth anchors saints in times of trouble, doubt, and sin in ways that feelings, which wax and wane, never can. Paul connects the singing of spiritual songs to letting "the word of Christ dwell in you richly" (Col. 3:16). Paul speaks of songs that "teach." When we rehearse the great truths of God, meditating and reveling in the multiple facets of the glorious gospel, we tune our hearts to what Christ has done for us, and this transforms our minds, our hearts, and our feelings into authentic worship of God.

Eating

The final component of biblical worship is . . . eating? In many evangelical churches, this final aspect of worship feels out of place, so let me unpack what I mean. Of course, it is important that Christians fellowship with one another and act hospitably to unbelievers. This is often described as "breaking bread" together. While this practice can be an important part of a gathering, and it is certainly a necessary part of the life of Christian community, what I have in mind is communion, sometimes called the Lord's Supper.

We tend to drift so easily into self-righteousness and treating others according to their merits. At regular intervals we need to "reset" ourselves. Recentering on the gospel in our weekly gathering recenters our community for day-to-day discipleship to Christ and fellowship with each other. We are reoriented toward Christ's glory in the worship service, like a skeletal alignment or an instrument recalibration.

The primary way this occurs is through the sermon. Preachers must preach the word contextually and Christocentrically (in a Christ-centered way) in order to make sure the gospel is of "first importance" during the teaching time. We devote ourselves to the apostles' teaching, following the pattern of the early church.

But we must also center on the gospel in our worship services through participation in the ordinances (or *sacraments* in some traditions). The first is baptism, intended for those making professions of faith. Baptism proclaims the covenant of grace by picturing Christ's death, burial, and resurrection. The second is communion in which we remember Jesus's atoning sacrifice and confess anew our Christian life in light of it. When we eat the Lord's Supper, we are not just remembering Christ's death, which gives us life; we are proclaiming it. "For as often as you eat this bread and drink the cup," Paul writes, "you proclaim the Lord's death until he comes" (1 Cor. 11:26). The ordinance of communion is a biblically prescribed way the church gathering remembers (and recenters on) the gospel.

Though many churches choose to celebrate communion infrequently, I believe that churches interested in being driven by the gospel should celebrate communion *as often as they can*. I don't think we have a clear enough word from Scripture to be dogmatic about the weekly exercise of communion, but I certainly think most churches rightly make that a goal. We certainly don't have biblical grounding for rare commemoration. I urge communion to be celebrated as frequently as possible, as it is an element of worship Jesus himself instituted.

Communion places us in a personal and corporate encounter with the sacrifice of Christ and presses us to meet God, confess our sin, and embrace afresh the gospel that saved us and continues to transform us. Churches practice communion in different ways, and I have my own opinions and preferences about the manner of celebration. The reason I mention the celebration of the Lord's Supper here is this: if your worship service is aimed at seekers, you will likely be missing out on this Christ-commanded sharing in the gospel message, the richest blessings of grace God has given us for worship. Although the lost cannot participate in communion, by seeing the believing and covenanting church partake, they see a picture of the gospel proclaimed—the blood and body of Christ given to unite sinners to God and to each other.

When we take care to "remember the gospel" in all our worship service elements, we focus on the only power that can truly change and sustain us. For those trained in an attractional paradigm, orienting the gathering around the edification of believers may seem counterintuitive, but it is not wrong to design our worship service to help, instruct, and equip the "already found." And we have to remember that this purpose is best accomplished by centering on the gospel that saves unbelievers. The beauty of gospel-driven worship is that it provides the best picture of biblical worship and the best opportunity for both the sanctification of Christians and the salvation of non-Christians.

We need to offer practical help or application in our teaching, but we cannot divorce such points from the central point of the finished work of Christ. Remember, we don't become more like Christ by focusing on dos and don'ts, but by focusing on the *done* of Christ's work.

The worship service shapes Christians both individually and as a community. Over time, the gospel-centered elements in our worship services and the regular rhythm of meeting together to remember the gospel will cultivate a community that treasures Christ. Gospel doctrine, songs, and all other manners that "rehearse the gospel" foster a gospel culture. And it is a gospel culture that glorifies God in Christ and overflows out into Spirit-empowered gospel mission.

In the following chapters, we will turn to the impact of the gospel on the church's experience of community (chapter 7) and our engagement in mission (chapter 8).

Messing with DNA

"You're the only one who understands me," Josh said.

Rob smirked. "Nah. Even I don't understand you."

"Well, then I'm really sunk."

"If it helps, I think things are clearing up. They're not anywhere close to clear. But the direction you took with Matt has showed us the radical nature of where we're going. I think when you become more settled on what this is, you'll see most of the others come along."

"I don't know about Matt."

"He might come along. But you're right; he's having the most trouble. I think it's because at first this impacts him the most. And he didn't have this revelation like you did. So until you're able to articulate it with more precision, he'll be in the dark and feel like he's bumping into things."

"I'm afraid it's me he wants to bump into."

"Ha. Well, I won't tell you that won't happen. But he's a good guy. Don't fault him for being where you were just last year."

"Oh, I don't," Josh said. "And you're right. I am learning not just where we ought to go but also some things about how to get us there. It's occurred to me that despite all the changes we've gone through since LifePoint was planted, none of them involved fundamentally reordering why we exist."

"You're flipping the script. No, that's not it. I know what you're doing. You're messing with DNA," Rob said.

Josh perked up. "Wow. Yeah. That's exactly what it is."

"Right now, you're just poking the church with a stick. But I bet the gamma rays are coming."

Josh nodded.

Rob said, "I hope you're ready for the fallout."

"Sure," said Josh. "But also, for the fall-*in*."

CHAPTER 7

Pressing the Gospel Reset on Church Community

Fostering a discipleship culture in your church

Rob was confused. "Fall-in?"

"Yeah," Josh said. "I know whatever we do will make waves, but I'm looking forward to seeing who gets excited, who gets on board. It could breathe new life into the church. In fact, if I'm right about the change in message, it will bring a lot of life to the church."

"Well, you know I'm with you. I mean, I don't really know where you're going! But I'm pretty sure I'm with you. You know I've been a little concerned all along with how what we do on the weekends translates to the rest of the week."

"I know. I'm sorry I've never really listened. To you or to Drake, really, who has similar concerns, I think."

"It's hard to argue with success," Rob said.

"Yeah. I think it's difficult for everybody to imagine we could be doing anything wrong given how much growth we've seen."

"And now you're talking about taking the risk of shutting that down."

Josh frowned. "I don't want to shut it down. If anything, I want to perk it up. What good is having thousands of people if they're not growing closer to Jesus and to each other?"

"You're speaking my language now," Rob replied.

"Tell me again what you see. I have the ears to hear!"

"You know we've always struggled getting people beyond the initial worship buy-in. We've troubleshot that to death. The number of people who progress beyond weekend attendance into our small group program or the Wednesday night training classes is, honestly, pitiful. Felix has a better turnout for volunteer services, but I think that's explainable for a couple of reasons. One, it's emphasized in the membership classes. Every member signs up for some kind of volunteer role. Also, we have a lot of nonmembers who serve, which we're all happy about, but it's a lower-cost investment. You can do it while you're here Sunday or on your own time otherwise. People like to feel useful too, of course. But getting them interested in growing spiritually or moving into community has been like pulling teeth."

"What's your take on why that is?" Josh asked.

"It fits pretty well with what our big survey showed. We do well at getting newer Christians and keeping newer Christians, but we're not doing great at inspiring them to want to grow or retaining the ones who do. I think, just like you do, that the weekend experience is the decoder ring. It tells them what to want."

"What do they want?"

"A weekly pick-me-up and some advice for how to live their 'real life.'" Rob replied.

"Church isn't their real life?"

"Obviously not."

Josh grimaced, but he knew Rob was right. The core constituency of LifePoint Church saw the church as a component of their life, not a vital center for it. And they had unwittingly fed right into this value. Their system was perfectly designed for the results they were getting— big crowd, low buy-in.

Rob continued, "Not to be clichéd, but we're a mile wide and an inch deep. We have set up the weekend experience to serve a certain kind of consumer, and we've never really challenged their consumerism. If anything, we've fed it. It doesn't even matter that you teach good content and use the Bible and that Matt leads them in songs about God. The whole thing has been designed to serve individuals, despite the huge crowd, and we've just fostered their individualism."

"Why didn't you tell me this five years ago!" Josh said, playfully punching Rob on the arm.

"Five years ago, I couldn't see it. I was new. I bought in. I thought leading a new groups program would help. But like you, I don't think programs work if people don't have a real desire for them. Wanting them to want them doesn't compute. We've shaped them not to want them."

"Yeah."

"The concern I raised a couple of years ago was about all the resources poured into the weekend. All the money, time, and people directed to the service—I thought it was short-shifting groups and eating up so much energy that people were too tired, in a way, to invest in another activity. I still think that's true, but it's not the whole truth."

"Somehow we have to begin emphasizing community on Sunday mornings."

"Yes. But not in, like, a new pitch for small groups. What you're doing with the teaching and the vision, what we might do with the music and the whole experience, the direction we go—all of that— might nurture a new appetite."

"Can you put some of this on paper? Not anything huge. Just some bullet points tracking your thinking here. It will help me process it and articulate it with others on the team. I'm glad you're here, Rob."

"Me too," Rob said. "Also, I don't think *fall-in* is a word."

Gospel-Centrality Nurtures a Culture of Grace

"An evident love for God and neighbor"—this is Jonathan Edwards's fifth mark of a genuine move of the Spirit of God. It is a key quality of a church that is being driven by the gospel. As Ray Ortlund says, "Gospel doctrine creates a gospel culture."[1] So if a culture of grace is not evident in our church, we have to consider the cause. Is our system set up to produce one?

The problem, as Pastor Rob puts it, is motivating people to *want* this. Everybody hungers for community whether they realize it or not. We were made for relationships with God and with other people. Because of sin and the fallenness of the world, however, we are not "discipled" well in our daily routines to fulfill this hunger in healthy, God-honoring ways. Many times, we seek to satisfy our need for belonging in sinful or otherwise dysfunctional ways, and the world around us only enhances our self-dependence. We swim in a sea of individualistic messages aimed at our consumeristic hearts.

When a church mirrors the values of the world outside by embracing the functional methodologies of pragmatism, consumerism, and legalism, we should not be surprised when congregants think of the church as the place where their individual desires are met (or not met), not as a place to unite with others in commitment and selfless service.

Countless churches try something new to program a sense of community within their congregations each year, but they rarely get a great turnout for their efforts. It's one of the major malfunctions of today's church, and I don't think it's accidental. Sure, there could be a problem with the programs being offered, that they are impractical, unwelcoming, or poorly led. But I believe that one important reason why churches struggle to develop biblical community is because so much of what the church does enhances the congregation's self-centeredness rather than challenging and confronting it. Nobody does this on purpose, of course! But when our messages and our music are aimed primarily at helping people live their best lives or addressing felt needs or experiencing some sort of spiritual euphoria to get them through their solitary week, we are training them—discipling them—in a way that is opposed to the kind of commitment to others to which the Bible calls them.

The gospel has the power to change this. It is perfectly equipped to nurture and empower its own implications, including stoking the desire in Christians for gospel-centered community. The message of grace in the gospel develops a culture of grace when a church is centered on the gospel. But the gospel doesn't create this desire for community unless believers take it seriously and apply the implications of the gospel to their lives.

It doesn't "just happen."

Instead, grace must be "fleshed out" in a variety of ways, and the intentional practice of applying the gospel to all of life will naturally, over time, make the impulse or habit of applying the gospel more reflexive. All this is facilitated supernaturally by God's Spirit, applying God's Word to the hearts, minds, and desires of God's people. Almost anybody with the right resources can draw a crowd. Growing the crowd spiritually takes the Spirit. And the Spirit prefers to use the means God has provided, not the worldly means employed by many churches today.

We clearly see in Acts 2:41–47 how the message of grace that made the church has also *shaped the church* into a culture of grace. The receiving of the word (2:41) transformed souls by grace into gospel-centered people who were devoted to each other. These individuals became a community and developed a culture of grace.

But how does the gospel do this? How does the gospel work in a church to develop a collection of individual Christians into a gracious community that takes the deep love of God seriously? The Bible is filled with instructions toward this end, not least of which are the "one another" passages we find throughout the Gospels and Epistles. Take a look at Romans 15:1–7, my favorite passage about the gospel shaping Christian community:

> We who are strong have an obligation to bear with the failings of the weak, and not to please ourselves. Let each of us please his neighbor for his good, to build him up. For Christ did not please himself, but as it is written, "The reproaches of those who reproached you fell on me." For whatever was written in former days was written for our instruction, that through endurance and through the encouragement of the Scriptures we might have hope. May the God of endurance and encouragement grant you to live in such harmony with one another, in accord with Christ

Jesus, that together you may with one voice glorify the God and Father of our Lord Jesus Christ. Therefore welcome one another as Christ has welcomed you, for the glory of God.

Notice the pattern revealed in these verses. The church can become anything God wants it to, but it *always starts with the gospel.* Verse 3 tells us what Christ did to save us, and verse 5 ascribes to God the credit in our graciousness, implying that these gospel truths drive the experience that follows. Verses 5–7, especially, give us a picture of what results when the gospel captivates a church community:

▶ There is harmony (v. 5).
▶ There is Spiritual growth (v. 5).
▶ There is unified worship (v. 6).
▶ There is gracious community (v. 7).

Don't miss this: all this results from the gospel. We must apply the gospel, and learn to do it well, if we want to shape our church this way. This process is often called *discipleship.*

Growth in Christ, Not Growth in Church

A couple of years ago, a friend in another city messaged me to share some frustrations he was having with his church experience. I didn't tell him this, but another friend, also an attendee of this church, had messaged me a few weeks prior with the same concerns. Both of these dear saints had left their previous churches, where they served well and participated fully, in order to join this new church plant downtown in their city. The church plant was founded with the sole purpose of reaching the lost. (Not a bad goal!)

The new church featured contemporary music led by capable musicians, better quality music and skilled musicians than they'd had at their previous churches. It featured a more dynamic preacher than their previous churches. And it was backed by a savvier media plan than their previous churches. As the church grew quickly, more than a few Christians left other churches in town to be a part of this new church, a church that was "finally making a difference."

I did not tell my friends this, but I could have predicted what they were sharing with me. I'm summarizing here, but this is, essentially, what they said to me: "I'm involved, I'm excited, and I believe in the mission. But I'm not growing." Both expressed shame in even saying that. They knew their new church was not really for them. It was for the lost. The whole endeavor was not predicated on discipling believers into maturity but simply getting seeking souls into the kingdom. They felt selfish and guilty expressing their frustration about their own lack of growth. In some attractional churches, anybody who raises this concern is seen as a problem, somebody who doesn't "get it," somebody who is self-centered or, worse, a legalist or a Pharisee challenging the church's evangelistic mission. My friends didn't feel they could express these concerns to their pastors for that very reason. They didn't know how the concerns would be received, if they would be ostracized or criticized, but they feared they might be rejected. To be clear, I am not saying every attractional church does this, only that it happens. And it's a problem.

As with many errors in the attractional paradigm, the frustration people experience is the result of a system that has forgotten what the church is really for. Reaching the lost, yes! But what about the need to facilitate growth in Christlikeness. A church that emphasizes evangelism *over* discipleship has not entirely understood the purpose of the church.

It may sound odd to many Christian leaders' ears to hear me say that discipleship matters. They may give me a puzzled look and say, "Of course it matters!" If you ask most Christian leaders what the whole point of Christian ministry is, nine out of ten will tell you "to make disciples." Yet we have a discipleship deficit in our churches. So it's not the result of people failing to take discipleship seriously. It's a failure to understand what biblical discipleship *actually is*. We're doing *something*, but what we're doing might not be discipleship.

Discipleship begins with evangelism, but it doesn't end there. Look at the authoritative commission for the church from Jesus himself:

"Go, therefore, and make disciples of all nations, baptizing them in the name of the Father and of the Son and of the Holy Spirit, teaching them to observe everything I have commanded you. And remember, I am with you always, to the end of the age" (Matt. 28:19–20 CSB). The Great Commission can be a tremendous help to us, not simply in evangelistic motivation but also in discipleship comprehension. Let's tease out a few reasons for the *discipleship deficit* found in many otherwise evangelistically minded churches by applying these words to the current evangelical landscape.

Discipleship Empowers Fidelity to Christ

Discipleship should lead to greater faith in Christ. I think people often miss that nuance in the Great Commission. Notice that Jesus didn't say simply to *make converts*; he said to *make disciples*. If evangelism consists of nothing more than "inviting Jesus into our heart" or "accepting Christ as our Savior," then we are not teaching people what it means to become a Christian. We are missing the *eternality* of conversion. Jesus instructs us to make disciples, and if the aim of our discipleship is getting people to pray the sinner's prayer, we are only partially obeying Jesus. And partially obeying Jesus is disobeying Jesus.

We may be good at accumulating a crowd or accumulating baptisms, but a better marker of faithfulness to the Great Commission might be a count of those who are coming to know Christ *and* being discipled. Discipleship can't end at the altar. Jesus did *not* say, "If anyone would follow me, he must pray this prayer." He *did* say, "If anyone would come after me, let him deny himself and take up his cross and follow me" (Matt. 16:24). Leaders, let's be faithful in evangelism and not neglect the call to proclaim the gospel to those lost and dying and going to hell, but let's also remember that Christ has called us not simply to make converts but to "make disciples."

Discipleship Ensures the Witness of the Church

Every time Barna, Gallup, or Lifeway releases the latest survey results on theological beliefs among confessing evangelicals, we see further slippage in those affirming the basic tenets of Christian ortho-doxy. Fewer people accept the exclusivity of Christ for salvation, the existence of hell, the infallibility of the Bible. Not only is our nation becoming less Christian, but the evangelical church is becoming less Christian. Moral relativism dominates our personal spirituality, therapeutic religion our theology, and consumeristic pragmatism our ministry.

A well-known female Christian author recently affirmed same-sex marriage, and thousands of Christians were fine with that. Ministers embrace worldliness, disqualifying themselves from the pastorate—at least according to biblical principles—and congregations hold them in higher esteem than the Word of God. The discipleship problem has huge implications for the integrity of the church's theology and the authenticity of its witness. We have seen what has happened to the mainline denominations as they continue to drift from God's Word and tailor their affirmations to the prevailing whims of the world. Let's not be so naïve and foolish as to think it could never happen to evangelicals.

Paul tells his young disciple, "Keep a close watch on yourself and on the teaching" (1 Tim. 4:16), and "What you have heard from me in the presence of many witnesses entrust to faithful men, who will be able to teach others also" (2 Tim. 2:2). This is what Jesus says in the Great Commission: "[Teach] them to observe *all* that I have com-manded you" (Matt. 28:20, emphasis added). Often Acts 2 is held up as a picture of the joyful fellowship of the early Christians, but remem-ber that they "devoted themselves to the apostles' teaching" (v. 42), which was essential to their joy and their growth.

I was once speaking to a crowd of Christian college students, and after my sermon a young man approached me to challenge my use of the phrase "Christ took the wrath of God." He wanted to argue against my affirmation of the penal substitution view of the atonement. While I don't think penal substitution is the only facet of Christ's atoning work, I do think it is the most important. My message wasn't about the theology of atonement. It was a basic gospel talk on Christ's extravagant grace to us. I didn't use the terms *atonement* or *penal sub-stitution*. Nevertheless, he picked up on my endorsement of this core Christian teaching about Christ's work on the cross and thought it was worthy of debate.

"I have a hard time believing in a vengeful God," he said. In his ensuing critique, he used the phrases "divine child abuse" and "bloodthirsty God." At first, I took him through some of the relevant Scripture passages, beginning in the Old Testament with the sacrificial system, proceeding through the messianic prophecy of Isaiah 53, straight into the garden of Gethsemane where Jesus refers to "the cup" (which most scholars recognize as a reference to God's wrath, including N. T. Wright, who is a favorite among penal substitution critics), and into some of the relevant passages in the Epistles.

He was unmoved, unconvinced.

Then it occurred to me to get personal. I asked him directly, "Are you a sinner?"

He paused for a second and finally said, reluctantly, "Yes."

So I said, "How is it that you are forgiven?"

He paused. Chewed on it. He looked up into the sky, as if heaven held the answer. (It does.) But he had no answer.

This Bible college student could not give me a reason for the hope he has within him. Why?

He'd heard the old gospel story, but at some point he found it irrelevant to his personal life and relationship with Christ. If I had to guess, knowing how some of the modern antagonism toward penal substitution spreads among young people today, somebody probably gave him a book that questioned the view. He had been discipled away from it. Consequently, not only could he not affirm the biblical teaching of Christ satisfying the wrath of God for sinners, he therefore could not see the personal value in Christ taking the wrath of God that was owed *to him*. The trajectory of his training led him to a place of theoretical Christianity, divorced from real, experiential Christianity. To put it more bluntly, his Christianity had become more academic than personal. He'd been discipled away from taking his faith personally.

And this is the reason large numbers of evangelicals today have no problem setting biblical teaching aside to affirm the idolatries of our culture or setting orthodoxy aside to flirt with repackaged modern heresies. Perhaps they said a prayer years ago, but they haven't been led to deny themselves, take up their cross, and follow Jesus. They haven't been discipled.

I am willing to bet that if many congregants knew what their leaders believed about same-sex marriage, for instance, they'd be shocked. That goes both ways. Some would be shocked that their cool pastors opposed it, for they have not been discipled according to Christian doctrine all that well. Others would be shocked that their leaders affirm it, because the church never teaches them to confront sin or progress beyond the realm of shallow inspirational living. If we want a strong church, one ready to weather the challenges of our increasingly post-Christian culture, we must take discipleship seriously.

Teach everything Jesus commanded, not just the appealing stuff. Teach the whole Bible to the whole church.

Discipleship Expands the Glory of God

"Go therefore and make disciples of all nations," Jesus says (Matt. 28:19). "I am with you always, to the end of the age" (v. 20). God's vision for the world is not primarily the bigness of the church but the bigness of his own manifest presence in every nook and cranny of the world. In Habakkuk 2:14, we see God's purpose-driven vision for everything:

> For the earth will be filled
> > with the knowledge of the glory of the LORD
> > as the waters cover the sea.

Could it be that one reason we see dwindling baptism numbers in some churches is because we've effectively turned "go and tell" into "come and see" and turned the long-view of missional expansion into the instant gratification of microwaved spiritual experience? One of the criticisms of the attractional movement is that by relegating evangelism to the Sunday morning service, we've embraced an understanding that a few experts are required to evangelize on Sunday mornings. Could this be the reason we aren't reaching many people with the gospel? Has the attractional church model inadvertently led us to abandon our mission?

While the "come and see" approach can win some lost people to Christ, it also disincentivizes and disempowers our people from being on gospel mission in their everyday lives. "Just bring them to church," we suggest, "we'll handle it." This reality is one of the reasons behind the rise of the missional movement in the early part of the twenty-first century. The missional movement acknowledges that attractional models of worship fail to disciple people and fail to challenge them to go into their communities with the gospel.

Most lost folks will not darken the door of our church building. We end up leaving the vast number of lost people unreached because we've trained our churches to behave as if the church service is the primary place for evangelism. This view not only misunderstands the biblical teaching on the point of the worship gathering, it also hamstrings our missional reach. Perhaps we'd baptize more on Sunday if we better discipled our people to share the gospel Monday through Saturday. Maybe our failure to disciple the converts we make is why we make fewer converts.

A church that focuses on "killer worship experiences" isn't preparing itself for God's coming and glorious global takeover. Our discipleship follows the self-sovereign and self-serving patterns of the world, yet we wonder why these disciples don't want to come together in loving community and loving mission.

That's why discipleship matters. That's why we can't settle for a big crowd. God's purposes are much bigger. God wants us to grow in devotion to Christ, not simply to grow our little churchly kingdoms. Jesus's dozen disciples in John 6 represent a much bigger kingdom force than the five thousand who came for a free meal.

Putting the Crowd in Order

As the gospel begins to shape a congregation's heart, leaders will need to be more intentional about facilitating the church's Spiritual growth. Even with gospel-centered preaching and music, gospel-centered community doesn't happen automatically. You may have stoked the desire for it, but you need a system to nurture it. Colin Marshall and Tony Payne call this "trellis work." We might also call it "applying the gospel *organizationally*." As we conclude this chapter, I want to share four key changes you can make to your church to nurture a gospel focus and develop a gospel culture.

Reevaluate Polity

One major—I mean really major—thing churches in transition ought to do is reevaluate their polity, by which I mean the local church's system of order, structure, and governance. For many congregations, not much tinkering can be done, especially if they are a part of certain denominations or are restricted by significant legalities in their bylaws or constitution.

Other churches have the freedom to consider how their structures might be inhibiting gospel growth. For instance, if your church makes a distinction between leaders called elders and leaders called pastors, why do you do this? What does this distinction serve? Does either group oversee the care of congregants? Is there a leadership bottleneck somewhere in the organization? Biblically speaking, the idea of "pastor" is synonymous with the biblical office of elder, so thinking through this division could help bring a church more closely alongside the Bible's portrait of healthy church leadership.

Churches with one pastor "at the top" enter precarious territory. We've all seen the cautionary tales of pastors who fall or otherwise exit such top-heavy contexts, and it is often difficult for churches to recover. When so much of the church revolves around one personality and one voice, the likelihood for a major disruption or even collapse of the church grows.

On the other hand, pastoral plurality, and parity, helps leaders share wisdom and perspectives, and it helps congregations see that decisions about significant change aren't one person receiving "a word from the Lord" but the result of the shared wisdom of a collaborative leadership. This doesn't mean that churches can't have a lead pastor, a primary teacher or vision-caster who serves as a sort of "first among equals" on a pastoral team or elder board, but it does mean that the lead pastor does not operate outside the accountability, insight, and cooperation of the other pastors of equal governing authority.

Is your church congregationally governed or elder governed? Thinking through the communication of significant change in a church can require different emphases depending on how much say the members have in decisions. I don't believe gospel-centrality requires a certain church polity. But anyone seeking to lead a church into closer community should at least consider the potential impact of the structure of the church. In my experience, the often-complex web of leaders, members, staff, decision-making policies, program implementation, hiring, firing, and other organizational distinctives have a direct impact on the church's ability to experience community or, for that matter, to make any significant paradigm shifts toward becoming gospel-driven.

Rethink Membership

This is not always the case, but in many attractional churches, there is no clear or meaningful understanding of membership. I attended an attractional megachurch for about ten years, and the membership process was primarily focused on recruiting and training volunteers to serve during the church service times. Two classes were required. One covered the church's doctrine, and the other covered the church's values, and the entire thing concluded with everyone taking a spiritual gifts inventory so the leaders could find out where to "plug you in."

Don't get me wrong, serving your church is a great thing! It's a necessary thing, in fact. It's never wrong to find ways to facilitate more involvement from the congregation in the workings of the church.

But I would argue that this is not the focus of church membership. To be honest, I was never a member of that church. It was never necessary for me to become one because, eventually, I was fairly well-known and my gifts for teaching and leading were recognized. I was authorized to lead groups and classes. I even taught the first part of the new members' class, despite the fact I wasn't a member!

I have learned that this practice is not a minority report, especially in churches that grow quickly and become large. Poor membership structures are not isolated to attractional churches, of course. There are plenty of churches, traditional and otherwise, that will accept anyone for membership who can articulate a few things about Jesus. Many don't have classes for teaching about the church and what they believe. You just say you're a Christian or say you're transferring from another church or say you want to be baptized, and you're in.

In such approaches, there is no real assessment of a prospective member's profession of faith or the fruit evidencing that faith in their lives. Further, while immediately assigning members to volunteer roles is admirable, the point of church membership should not be to get to the "next level" of church buy-in. Church membership should require you to covenant with other Christians, to promise to represent the church well, and to submit to the oversight and care of the church leaders.

The greatest deficiency in attractional church membership structures is that members are not adequately or appropriately *pastored*. Members come and go, just like "normal" attendees, and nobody knows when or why members leave. Members may engage in grievous sin, which brings their profession into question or stains the witness of the church, and nobody helps them repent. Few faithful sheep are shepherded, and wayward sheep are rarely, if ever, disciplined.

This disorder is antithetical to the gospel. The gospel creates order among God's people and inspires the watchful care of others. If there is no meaningful shepherding for those who join the church, it becomes frustratingly difficult to find and experience the honest, transparent, deep community that shapes us by the gospel.

If our leaders don't care for us in personal, relational ways, why would we care for others that way?

Reorder Small Groups

The kind of small group structure your church facilitates is not as important as what actually happens in the groups. I believe we have a lot of leeway in *when* or *where* we spend our time together, but only a little leeway in *how* we spend our time together. There is no hard-and-fast rule for how gospel-centered group time should be conducted, but there are a few elements that are often missing from church small group programs.

Most groups have "hang time" down pat. It is wonderful to hang out with brothers and sisters in Christ. Yet the purpose of community is not solely for fellowship, at least not in the superficial sense of just hanging out. Our groups can easily be missing depth, like the depth that comes from mutual confession. We must be vulnerable with each other in order to see how powerful the gospel can be in our lives. Of course, transparency can go awry, with group time becoming a spiritualized therapy session. That's not the aim. That being said, we should leave space for messiness and inefficiency so that we can learn to drop the pretense that we are highly functional people and begin to see each other's real selves. We do this not so that we can gossip or gloat but so that we can see the grace of God take greater influence in our community.

The most transformative book I have read—that isn't God's inspired Word—is Dietrich Bonhoeffer's classic work on the experience of Christian community, *Life Together*. In it, Bonhoeffer comments on the need for community time to facilitate gospel encounters between brothers and sisters. He urges us to approach community as real and receptive people. Why?

> The Christ in his own heart is weaker than the Christ in the word of his brother; his own heart is uncertain; his brother's is sure.

And that clarifies the goal of all Christian community: they meet one another as bringers of the message of salvation.[2]

When community groups are centered on the gospel, they provoke us to know, confess to, receive, and even sharpen each other.

Pastor Jeff Vanderstelt tells a story about a friend who disrupted the carefully laid plans for their missional community:

We had several friends who regularly joined us for our weekly missional community meals. Some of these people did not yet share our faith in Jesus. One evening, Josh and his wife, Dana, participated in a discussion with some of our neighbors who had yet to trust in Jesus. Throughout the night, Josh aggressively argued, counterargued, and cornered one particular couple. The following week, this couple was obviously missing from our weekly meal together. Jayne called them to find out why they hadn't joined us, and they informed her that they no longer wanted to be a part of our weekly meal. When she asked why, they shared that they had been deeply hurt by how Josh had treated them. At first, Jayne and I wanted to nail Josh. We were angry with him for ruining our mission to our neighbors. Then the Spirit reminded me: "This is the work. You are called to disciple Josh as much as your neighbors."[3]

Sometimes people get in the way of the vision, until you realize the vision must include people. Even the messy ones. *Especially* the messy ones.

The experience of gospel community allows us to see things in each other we cannot see ourselves. Again, this is not so we can find out who the real losers are, but so that we can find out that we are all equally losers! And so that we might, as Luther says, join together as beggars pointing each other to where we've found bread.

Gospel-centered community inevitably includes the confession of sin. Because the gospel's primary aim is dealing with sin, we should expect that any ordering of community should include the loving, biblical confrontation of sin. James certainly thought so: "Therefore, confess your sins to one another and pray for one another, that you may be healed. The prayer of a righteous person has great power as it is working" (James 5:16). Bonhoeffer says, "In confession, the breakthrough to community takes place."[4] Confession takes great care and patience on the part of the group, as well as mature leaders who are wise beyond the basic training of being able to read through some study questions or put out the chips and dip.

These leaders should also be able to do some basic teaching of the Bible, or at least be able to competently facilitate good discussion about the Bible, ask probing questions, prompt self-reflection, prevent wonky exegesis, and gently correct (real) errors. Small group leaders don't need to be scholars or pastorally qualified people, but they should be more than hospitable extroverts. Because the gospel is the most important thing we can hear in these groups, group leaders should be able to articulate it well, along with its myriad implications. This means, of course, the leaders have some training.

Recruit and Replicate Disciple-Makers

Church communities should be led well by those who have been led well. Part of making disciples is making disciples who make disciples. If you do not have a discipleship plan in your church, you are not planning to make disciples.

Functionally, this can look like a lot of different things. But it begins with a concerted effort to identify leaders and those with leadership potential. Potential leaders might be discovered through the incoming membership process, through the ministry of pastoral care, and throughout the normal life of the church. Existing leaders should be discipling emerging leaders to the point of maturity when they can "pay it forward" with another set of emerging leaders.

Every leader in your church should have a set of disciples, even if it's just two or three. One of the best resources I know of to help pastors and leaders think through who to start with and how to start with them is Marshall and Payne's *The Trellis and the Vine*, in which they write:

> [The] transfer of the "good deposit" of the gospel is not a barren, educational exercise. It's deeply and inescapably relational. When we look at the relationship between Paul and Timothy, it becomes immediately apparent that much more than a transfer of skills or information was involved in Timothy's training. Paul repeatedly describes Timothy with great warmth as his son and beloved child (1 Cor 4:17; Phil 2:22; 1 Tim 1:2; 2 Tim 1:2, 2:1). Timothy was almost certainly converted through Paul's ministry (Acts 14:6–23, 16:1–3), and became a highly valued co-worker in the gospel mission ("I have no-one like him"—Phil 2:20), whom Paul trusted to send as his emissary to the churches (Phil 2:19–20; 1 Thess 3:1–5).
>
> This close relationship was a vehicle for one of the key elements of Paul's training of Timothy—imitation.[5]

Discipleship does not happen by osmosis. Nor does it happen "organically," at least not in the unintentional, accidental sense.

These discipleship relationships don't have to be overly formal. I think of the times I was most impacted by leaders who mentored me, like my first pastoral mentor Mike Ayers, who taught me much and gave me leadership opportunities. Mike let me shadow him during his regular ministry routines. I followed him as he followed Christ. I also think of my favorite youth pastor when I was a teenager, Chris Trent. Even though I was a pimply junior high student, he took my aspiration to ministry seriously. He gave me plenty of instruction and let me on the student ministry team that was made up mostly of high schoolers. Many of the most profound moments I shared with Chris, however, occurred riding around in his truck running errands, hanging out at his house with his family, or accompanying him to McDonald's for some weeknight evangelism.

The key to this kind of discipleship is intentionality and relational proximity. But you can conduct these training moments formally too, and you should. At Liberty Baptist Church, I direct the Pastoral Training Center, which is an eighteen-month residency program for those pursuing a call to vocational ministry. We have monthly three-hour group meetings, where we work through some teaching, book discussions, prayer, and Q&A coaching. The formal meeting times are complemented by multiple one-on-one times over lunch or coffee. I often take residents with me when I travel to preach. The relational times reinforce the group training times, and vice versa.

Through this discipleship program, we gain a pool of teachers for small groups or theology classes and new preachers for our pulpit and others'. More than that, we help equip a group who will be qualified to lead churches and equip others. At the end of the eighteen months, I start again with another group.

Your process depends on your context and the available resources. But you must have a process to recruit and then replicate disciple-makers. Your effort in discipling others strengthens the life of the church and helps the church experience the gospel. We are applying the gospel organizationally in order that we might delight in it more corporately.

The goal, of course, is that our gospel-shaped community will become a gospel-driven community, ready to serve not their own interests but the interests of others, including those who don't yet know Jesus.

CHAPTER 8

Moving toward Mission

Turning the corner from "Come
and see" to "Go and tell"

I wondered when you were gonna get to us."

Drake leaned back in his chair and folded his arms, pretending to be smug and unreceptive. His smirk gave it away. And so did the fact that Sandy couldn't keep a straight face.

Josh said, "I'm sorry."

Drake said, "We forgive you, I think."

"Look," said Josh, "I know you've both probably felt out of the loop. It made more sense for me to be working through some of the big picture stuff with the pastors, just so I could get more clarity on it. But we couldn't keep your name out of our conversations, Drake. All along I've known I need to bring you both into the discussion as quickly as possible. Now that I think I know what we're doing, I want to get your input on the impact it could have on your areas."

Sandy asked, "And what is it that we're doing?"

"We are going to reboot LifePoint. We're going to repurpose the church around a bigger focus on Jesus."

Sandy replied, "My guess is you've already had people say that we already focus on Jesus."

"Well, yeah. Mostly Bob and Matt. And that's been mainly because of my inability to articulate it. LifePoint has always 'been about Jesus.' What else would we be about? But when you start looking through how our vision plays out in the service and beyond, it becomes clear that Jesus is sort of just one of the things we do."

"I know," Drake said.

Josh smiled, hung his head a little. He and Drake had an interesting history. Josh hired Drake, the student minister, on the recommendation of a friend from seminary and based on Drake's obvious teaching gifts. But the kid had been a squeaky wheel all along. Drake was easily the smartest guy in any room, at least as it pertained to theology. And the problem was, he knew it. He was also constantly at odds with the LifePoint culture. Not individual people. There was no relational conflict between Drake and anybody else, at least not as far as Josh knew. But Drake seemed to wear how ill-fitted he was for LifePoint on his shirtsleeves.

Drake represented a different tribe, really. He didn't like the same books as everybody else or find the same influencers as helpful. He didn't go to the same conferences as everybody else, unless Josh made him. He listened to different podcasts, followed different people on Twitter. (Josh sometimes wondered if Drake's retweets of particular accounts were passive-aggressive "subtweets" criticizing LifePoint.)

In Josh's previous way of thinking, this wasn't really a huge deal. He remembered what it was like to be in his twenties. He remembered what it was like to think you knew more than your elders, especially older pastors who you felt were stuck in their ways. In a lot of ways, LifePoint started as a way to finally "do church right." So he let a lot slide.

Really, Josh let a lot slide because he didn't think student ministry was all that important. He certainly didn't think it was as important as most parents of teenagers did. He figured all Drake was doing was getting some ministry experience in a low-impact department, and in a few years, he would move on anyway. Drake really needed to be a lead pastor somewhere. He just had some growing up to do.

Plus, he was a pretty funny guy. Drake wasn't a jerk. He was just annoying sometimes.

It was especially annoying at this moment because Josh suspected

Drake had been right about a lot of his concerns all along, and Josh was the jerk for not loving him enough to ask him for his insights.

"The problem is," Josh repeated, "we have—I have—talked a lot about Jesus without really showing Jesus. I'm learning how to do that better in my preaching. I'm working with Matt on how to do that with our music and other creative elements. It's not enough for us to have Jesus as a character in the worship service. He needs to be the point. And not just in the 'it's all about Jesus' clichéd way. I am pouring over all our worship service content right now to make sure it communicates clearly and explicitly the truths of Jesus and the good news. I think, over time, this worship reboot will have positive effects on the church as a whole. At least, I'm assuming it will, since I've always assumed Sunday mornings mattered and affected the church as a whole. Otherwise we wouldn't do them!

"But I want to bring everything in line with this vision too. A refocus on Jesus. I've been talking with Rob about our problems getting people involved with community. We think the rebooted service will help in the long run, but in the short term, we are working through reordering how we train leaders and how groups are run. But I want to go deeper, especially with some of the more complex ministries. That's why I asked you two to this meeting."

Sandy said, "Can I just pause you for a second? It's not often that anyone refers to what we do as complex."

"Well," Josh said, "it is. I know that. It's why I don't wade into those waters too much myself!"

"What's complex about student ministry?" Drake said. "We just eat pizza and play video games."

"You and Sandy have maybe the two most difficult ministries in the church. You have to babysit all the grown-ups' idols."

"Now you've already ruined it," Sandy said playfully. "Calling what we do babysitting. I already have plenty of parents who expect my team simply to be the church's daycare service."

"No, I don't mean babysitting kids. Babysitting idols. These kids are their parents' objects of worship way too often. Which is why you two are in the most difficult positions at the church. Any decision you make gets scrutinized and criticized because you're messing with people's kids. So the first thing I want to know is what you think of our plan to refocus on Jesus. Then I want to know how you think that would work out in your ministries. And then I want to know what the response might be from your customers—oops, I mean, parents."

Sandy laughed. "I can answer the first question. It's easy for us, because we've already been focusing on Jesus. And not in the way LifePoint has always thought it was. We use curriculum with all age groups that is gospel-centered, teaching the Bible stories in a way that Jesus is the star of the show. With older kids, we teach more basic doctrinal truths, adapting a children's catechism for easier use with volunteer teachers. I wouldn't have said this to you a year ago, but the children's ministry is the most gospel-centered department at LifePoint. These kids get more gospel than their parents, to be honest."

Josh was impressed. And surprised. "Oh wow. Why didn't I know this?"

"Like you said," replied Sandy. "You don't wade into these waters. There have been plenty of times that I wished you and the other pastors took more interest in what we do, gave us more guidance. But one of the benefits of being left to run the ministry as we see fit has been enjoying the freedom to teach as I think best. And because it's kids, of course, it is low-impact on the culture of the church, because the kids don't really know that what they get here is different from what Mom and Dad are getting in the worship experience."

Drake said, "She's been creating an army of little gospel-centered soldiers right under your nose. The future of LifePoint!"

"And you would have gotten away with it if it weren't for your snooping pastor."

Sandy beamed. "Honestly, I just wanted these kids to get what I didn't get in church growing up, which is the reassurance that God loved me no matter what. They might have said that, but so much of the teaching was on being good, being brave, being right, that it left me with the impression that my Christian life hung a lot on how I performed. That wasn't the intention. But it was the effect. So I want to get these kids as much gospel as possible, with—yeah—the hope that they will grow up, and the ones who are still here might change things. Assuming Drake and his crew don't run them out."

"I'm really good at that," Drake quipped.

"All of that is to say," said Sandy, "I'm open to guidance and leadership on this, but we are doing it already. In terms of impact, I don't think our ministry will feel too much of that. At this stage, even though parents may make idols of their kids, there's not a scrutiny of what's being taught out of fear the kids won't want to know God or whatever. That starts when they're teenagers."

"Okay," Josh said. "Tell me about that, Drake."

Drake craned over their meeting table, getting serious. Josh could tell he'd been waiting to have this conversation for a long time.

"I am more hamstrung on this than Sandy," Drake said. "It is more visible what we do in student ministry, for one thing. Teens have more options. Kids are here because parents are here. That's not true for most of my teenagers. They may be here out of parental pressure, but the older they get, the more pressure of their own they exert. And the more vocal they get. If they find youth group boring, cheesy, unhelpful, or *whatever*, they tell their parents or they just peace-out. And, like Sandy said, as the kids get older, their parents start to worry more about how spiritual they are: if they'll go to church while they're away at college, if they believe in Jesus, or if they just did that because Mom and Dad expected them to. Parents worry about all the outside influences. So the pressure is big to keep them here, keep them happy, keep them excited."

"That sounds exhausting," Josh said.

"It sucks. Because I don't have 2,500 students. We lose some from the worship service, we don't notice as much. Or more wander in to replace them. In the student ministry, everybody sees, everybody knows. So if Patsy Popular decides youth group is stupid and bails, guess what? So do eight of her friends and four girls who wish they were her friends."

"Patsy Popular?"

"She's a real girl," Drake said, finally joking again. "Look her up."

"Okay," said Josh. "And the impact of changing?"

"We're already feeling it. You know I do enough of the rock show and games to keep the criticism as much at bay as possible, but I do straight Bible teaching. We've transitioned our classes to same-gender small groups aimed at more intensive discipleship and accountability. I train my leaders to talk about real issues and apply the Bible to them. More than a few kids like it, a few parents don't mind it, but for everybody else, it's like they're just beginning to smell a fart in the room."

"You know," Josh said, "sometimes I think you're the most brilliant guy we've got. And then you remind me you're just the youth guy."

"Well, it's true. You may not know what exactly we do, but I know you get emails and phone calls about it. Our church is three times the size of Cedar View Baptist, but their student ministry is three times the size of ours. Not to knock on them, but they've got a boring church service but, as the kids say"—he made finger quotes—"a rockin' youth ministry."

"I'm sorry I haven't been more supportive," Josh said.

"Oh, it's mostly fine. I know that what I want to do isn't everybody's thing. And especially here, given our culture, where I've wanted to go with the student ministry was basically like creating a different culture within the culture. So my take on the response question you asked is this: if we reboot the church, which I assume means I can go full tilt gospel in student ministry, we will see people leave in droves."

Josh sat there for a few seconds, not saying anything. Drake was the first person to put it so starkly. He and the other pastors knew that any big transition brought some attendance fallout; it happens to any church making any significant change. But nobody said people would leave in droves.

"Assuming that's true," Josh said, "what points of emphasis would you make for whoever remains?"

"My take," said Drake, "is that we're not adequately preparing students, and I think also the regular attenders of LifePoint, for how the world really is. Most of the teaching they get—no offense—assumes they live in some Christian cultural bubble or at the very least that Christian cultural bubble advice will help them with lost friends and family. My kids are asking bigger questions than even my generation was asking. And the answers they get at church aren't equipping them to navigate well. If it were up to me, I'd be thinking about our church more in terms of mission. How do we prepare our people, and our church as a whole, to live every day 'confidently sent' as missionaries and not as individual religious journeymen?"

"I see," Josh said. "It's a similar concern Rob and I shared about how LifePoint has unintentionally fostered individualism."

"Right," said Drake. "How do we influence our people to move from cultural consumers to cultural missionaries?"

From "Come and See" to "Go and Tell"

A church centered on the gospel of Jesus Christ will be turned inside out because the gospel rightly grasped compels a church to join God's mission in the world.

Local churches should exist as "missional outposts" in their neighborhoods and cities. Churches must be places of spiritual refuge, doctrinal education, and ministry equipping. Attractional churches exist almost solely as "people in place"—a place people come for equipping and teaching. The church must gather as a congregation, but the church gathering is only one front in the mission, and it is not necessarily the most effective configuration. The church as "people in place," a gathering together in a physical building once a week, best serves those who are professing Christians and those drawn by the community to investigate more of the claims of the gospel. With few exceptions, the church as "people in place" struggles with evangelism.

What the attractional church gets right is the mission to seek and save the lost. But much of the execution of the attractional paradigm inverts the seeker mindset. In the attractional paradigm, it is not Christ through his church seeking the lost, but the lost seeking Christ through his church. Certainly, some unbelievers become genuine seekers by *seeking* a church. A few will hunt for a "people in place" to seek spiritual guidance. But most unbelievers would never step into a church building or attend a church event.

The attractional church has taken the evangelistic and revivalist rallies of the mid-twentieth century and given them a fog-and-lasers makeover. Attractional churches say, "Just get your friends here. We'll get them saved." While that approach *can* be successful, it is neither culturally aware nor biblically patterned. Acts and the Epistles depict a church that gathered regularly, in part, as a rest and rejuvenation for the mission they were engaged in the rest of the week. The early church welcomed unbelievers who visited their worship gatherings— they were appropriately "seeker sensitive"—but they did not orient those gatherings around unbelievers. Instead, they viewed the work of evangelism and outreach as taking place in their lives outside the weekly worship gathering.

Transitioning from an attractional mindset to a missional mind-set means understanding that the church isn't simply "people in place" but also "people in place*s*," plural. It prioritizes the missional strategy of "go and tell" over "come and see." For many attractional church-goers, the experience of church is simply the weekend worship service, an event to which they might bring a lost friend or family member. These congregants are not motivated or trained to share the gospel with unbelievers. If they are inclined to share the gospel, they know it only ever gets as hard as inviting someone to church. For missional, gospel-centered churchgoers, being the church becomes central to their identity. Being the church encompasses the weekend gathering and daily life, as Christians maintain life together through community and mission. Evangelism becomes less concentrated on a church event and more mobilized through the church's way of life.

Some of this thinking derives from how Christians have been trained to do evangelism (when they have been trained to do evangelism). The kind of evangelism training I received sounded like a sales pitch. This evangelism had rhetorical gamesmanship to it, which was reinforced with a heavy dose of guilt for falling short on my witnessing quota. My evangelism training came from the *Glengarry Glen Ross* school: ABC, "always be closing," or else you're out on your keister.

Okay, I'm exaggerating, but not much.

Many church people are familiar with the call of Jesus, "I will make you fishers of men," and they've been led to think of evangelism like baiting a hook to lure a lost person into the church boat. (To be filleted and eaten? I'm not sure.) Seen this way, it makes sense to think of church as a place of enticement and attraction. Get people in the door, and they'll hear about Jesus.

In the sales world, we call that the "bait and switch."

Is that what Jesus meant when he called his disciples to be "fishers of men"? For one thing, fishermen in those days didn't typically use hooks. They used nets. For another, it's not likely that Jesus was trying to make a neat correlation between literal fishing and reaching the lost. He was trying to get fishermen to consider how they might serve the mission of God in the midst of their everyday life (including in their job as fishermen). In other words, Jesus was not giving us an evangelism technique but a missional mandate. And this mandate becomes clearer to a church as the gospel becomes clearer. As Joel Lindsey says,

> Primarily, a missional church recognizes the centrality of the gospel as its people live out the calling to be "for" the culture. This means a church must derive its purpose from the gospel (1 Corinthians 15:1–4); it must be a servant of the gospel that glorifies God by telling people the story of Jesus through word and action (1 John 3:16–17). A gospel-centered church's ministry cannot be separated from the person of Jesus, nor can its mission be defined or performed apart from the gospel. The gospel is the ultimate guide and authority for how the church functions and ministers. Said another way, a missional church embraces God's call to be a sender of missionaries to its own culture (Matthew 4:19; Acts 16:20; 17:6).[1]

The attractional paradigm only sees the promise of Jeremiah 29:11: "For I know the plans I have for you, declares the LORD, plans for welfare and not for evil, to give you a future and a hope." The missional paradigm sees all of Jeremiah 29, helpfully summarized by verses 5–7: "Build houses and live in them; plant gardens and eat their produce.... But seek the welfare of the city where I have sent you into exile, and pray to the LORD on its behalf, for in its welfare you will find your welfare."

The chart below contrasts the core features of attractional and gospel-driven mission. Admittedly, this paints the two views with a broad brush, and not every church that fits into either label will possess all the qualities listed. But I think it gives a helpful thirty-thousand-foot perspective on how the paradigms are different.

Attractional Mission	Gospel-Driven Mission
Church as people in place	Church as people in place and people in places
Seeker-targeted gathering	Seeker-mindful gathering
Evangelism inside	Evangelism outside
Programmatic	Communal
Mission as program (event-driven)	Mission as purpose (missional)
Pragmatic	Exegetical
Growth is numbers	Growth is health
Complex	Simple
Culturally relevant	Culturally engaged
Institutional and rigid	Adaptable and flexible
Worship as attraction	Worship as response
Preaching as application	Preaching as proclamation
Weekend as experience	Weekend as assembly
Gospel as feature	Gospel as center

While gospel-centered churches should be missional, not every missional church is necessarily gospel-centered. Yet the attractional church is fundamentally at odds with gospel-centrality. In place of the attractional model, a gospel focus should lead us back to God's mission of going out into the world.

If an attractional church transitioning to gospel-centrality wants to become more missional, what can it do, practically speaking? Like community, mission occurs in response to the gospel, but it does not occur on autopilot. What makes it happen?

Since changing the message changes the movement, we should expect that the content of our preaching would "steer from the stage" a shift of this magnitude.

Gospel-Centered, Missional Preaching

If our Sunday preaching isn't an evangelistic crusade, in what sense might gospel-centered preaching serve the missional impulse in our church? There are at least five ways to focus your preaching on the gospel mission.

Put the Text in the Context of God's Mission

The Bible has a metanarrative, a grand story of God's redeeming purpose and Spiritual mission in the earth. We often miss this grand story in our preaching and teaching. Help your hearers make the connection between the narrative you are preaching and the big story of God's mission. This will help them begin to see their own story in the context of the big story of God's mission. Make regular, explicit application of biblical texts to their missional contexts, drawing out their missional implications, and this helps influence hearers to begin to think in missional ways.

Make Application Mission-Oriented

Rather than limiting the application of your sermon to individualistic activities or steps, make the practical admonitions you share "others-directed." Help people see that applying the Scriptures to everyday life is not about living their best life now. Nor is it something they do by themselves. Applying Scripture to life is about loving and serving others, especially those they encounter at work, school, and in public places.

Confront Idols

One of the most important things a local church can do is exegete its community and the culture of its city in order to identify the predominant idols. Preachers should contextualize their preaching to address these idols. The people of your church need this. These idols are their greatest temptations away from God. Explicating how the gospel subverts and conquers specific idolatries in your context can (1) help lost people present in the room encounter God, (2) help Christians in the room repent, and (c) train the Christians in the room to identify and address the effects of idolatry in their daily lives and mission.

Anticipate the Right Questions

Just as missional preaching can confront the idols of the church's mission field, it can also anticipate the spiritual, theological, ethical, biblical, or personal questions lost people may bring into the gathering with them. At the risk of redundancy: this doesn't mean the sermon should be aimed at the lost, but it does mean the sermon should be appropriately seeker-sensitive—meaning, it should be mindful of lost people in the room, *including people who think they are Christians.* Think ahead of time about addressing objections, questions, and obstacles that may lie between them and the gospel.

Pastors Tim Keller and Andy Stanley anticipate these questions well. They have different ways of addressing the objections they anticipate, but both should be admired and appropriately emulated for having the presence of mind in their preaching not to take understanding of theological truths for granted. Trevin Wax writes,

These two pastors come from different contexts (Atlanta vs. New York) and different theological streams (Baptist non-denominational vs. confessional Presbyterian). What's more, they approach ministry from different starting points, then employ different methods to achieve their purposes.

Despite all these differences, there is one thing Stanley and Keller agree on: *preachers ought to be mindful of the unbelievers in their congregation.* . . .

Stanley and Keller may be worlds apart in terms of their theological vision for ministry, but they both maintain that a preacher should consider the unsaved, unchurched people in attendance.

This doesn't mean we can't find differences even in this area. For example, Stanley uses the terminology of "churched" and "unchurched" (which makes sense in the South), whereas Keller's context leads him to terms like "believers" and "non-believers."

Likewise, Stanley and Keller engage in similar practices from different vantage points. Stanley's purpose for the weekend service is to create an atmosphere unchurched people love to attend. Keller believes evangelism and edification go together because believers and unbelievers alike need the gospel. He writes:

"Don't just preach to your congregation for spiritual growth, assuming that everyone in attendance is a Christian; and don't just preach the gospel evangelistically, thinking that Christians cannot grow from it. Evangelize as you edify, and edify as you evangelize."

Whether you are closer to Stanley's paradigm for ministry or Keller's, you can benefit from [their example of] how to engage the lost people listening to you preach.[2]

Anticipating the right questions, like confronting idols, trains your believing audience to know the answers to the questions they encounter on a daily basis in their homes, workplaces, schools, and online. You are equipping them for mission on the primary front even as you preach to "people in place."

Give the Motivation of Grace

The gospel is the power of salvation. That means that the gospel is also the power for missional engagement. The quickest way to shut down your church's missional response to the gospel is to leverage guilt in motivating them to reach their lost friends. Turning it into a competition, shaming people who fall short, playing on their fears or insecurities, and being overly critical do not encourage people to joyfully follow Christ in mission. These practices demotivate people to share the gospel. Remember that the gospel will empower on its own. So remind your "people in place" when they are serving as a "people in places" that they have all the wind of the Spirit at their backs, that God has always been roaming the earth seeking whom he may revive, that the kingdom is not contingent upon them but upon him, and that they are responsible for evangelistic faithfulness, not evangelistic success.

The motivation of grace better triggers a church's impulse for gospel mission.

Not every sermon can do all these things, of course, and quite a few sermons don't do any of them. But if you want to change the movement, you have to change the message. Therefore, a regular practice of preaching from the gospel-centered paradigm with a missional mindset can help shape a church for being on mission.

Missional Molding

As part of your system of disciple-making, Bible education, and community experience, you'll want to scatter missional seed in each of these areas. Everything we previously said about nurturing a discipleship culture is also in play for nurturing a missional culture. The two go hand in hand since the Bible teaches that making disciples means *making disciples who make disciples*. Replication is an inherent part of the system, and this is, by definition, what it means to live on mission. Churches can be shaped into a more missional form by offering training, engaging together, leading by example, repurposing your programs, commissioning community groups, and planting churches.

Offer Training

Your people need intentional, direct training on how to share the gospel, how to respond to challenges and questions from critics and skeptics, and how to become more hospitable and servant-minded in their neighborhoods. We can no longer expect people to "just know" how to do this. Nor, as I've said, can we expect the bulk of evangelistic effort to be inviting someone to church. As Collin Hansen says, "If you're a commissioned Christian, you know that we cannot simply expect neighbors to show up in church."[3] This is increasingly true *in every context*.

You will have lost people in your services, but if your evangelistic strategy turns people into recruiters for your weekend gathering, you may get a big crowd, but you are truncating the mission and stunting your people. Help your people be on mission outside the four walls of your church building. Make your church's missional reach that much wider and, honestly, more effective.

What does evangelism training look like in a gospel-centered church?

Evangelistic techniques can be helpful, but scripted presentations are becoming less and less effective in most contexts. It doesn't mean we can't employ them; it just means they are not as productive a means of adorning the gospel as they used to be.

Evangelism training in the church reminds us that the gospel is power for salvation and that no evangelist is responsible for someone's conversion, only for their having heard the gospel.

Your churches should also provide adequate training in apologetics and worldview. In our rapidly pluralizing world, we cannot assume that most of the unbelievers we share the gospel with will have a basic understanding of Christianity, or an awareness of spiritual things at all. But those who have a basic understanding are more likely than ever to issue objections. Our culture's latent knowledge of Christianity is eroding.

It would also be helpful to coach your missional people in the way of emotional intelligence. There is no replacement for the content of the gospel which bids a sinner to repent and believe. There is no getting around that. However, the church needs more evangelists who are more likely to love people and intuit their doubts, concerns, and challenging contexts than they are to debate or rhetorically corner them with an evangelism presentation. We can win some if we're winsome.

In general, sent people need a gracious community to serve as a "home base." This is another reason why gospel-centrality is so crucial to the experience of church. Evangelism as the church's mission is superior to evangelism as a personal project. When we have the prayer and preaching support of our church, we are bolder in our evangelism. When we have a community that is hospitable, welcoming, and ready to receive seekers, we have more than just a personal faith to call people into with our evangelism; we have a redemptive family that has been made by the gospel we're sharing.

Engage in the Mission Together

Opportunities for "missional molding" can vary between churches and among contexts. They might include justice efforts in your city, evangelistic outreaches, service at homeless shelters or soup kitchens, adopting a nearby school and serving teachers and students there, opening up a coffee shop (outside of your church building) to serve the community and facilitate gospel-centered cultural engagement. The point is that you provide avenues of mission for your church and that you do it together.

This does not mean your focus should be exclusively local. Your church should support mission partners (both across town and across the globe). Fund missions work, become supporters of specific missionaries, and have them come speak in your church while on furlough. Keep the church up to date on their efforts. If possible, send foreign missionaries from your own congregation to unreached and unengaged people groups. Keep God's mission in the world in front of your church's eyes.

Be an Example

You cannot tell people to be on mission if you cannot show them what it looks like. Preacher, do any of your personal stories have to do with evangelistic encounters or engagement with seekers or skeptics? Do you embrace the church's organized opportunities for service in the world? Do you host lost people in your home for meals and conversations? Do you show hospitality to strangers? Do you support missionaries and missions work? Do you serve your community? In your discipleship efforts, do those you are training get an opportunity to accompany you on mission in your day-to-day life?

Don't just tell—*show*. What the leadership is, the church will become.

Remember that a "missional program" will not by itself create the desire in your church to join God's mission. Colin Marshall and Tony Payne write,

> Now the temptation is simply to "run the course"—by directing your small groups to do it, or by issuing a general invitation for interested people to show up. And having run a group or groups of people through the course, you can pat yourself on the back for having done some "training." And there is no question that working through this material will be of benefit to those involved. However, to make real progress in helping the Christians in your congregation become "encouragers," they need more than a six-week course. They need the example of seeing it done; and they need the personal instruction and mentoring and prayer that addresses the spiritual issues at the heart of becoming an "encourager." This takes time and personal attention—before, during, and after the structured training opportunity.[4]

Lead by example.

Repurpose Programs or Structures

One of the things that inevitably comes up during big transitions is whether to cut unnecessary or outdated programs. An even more difficult issue is how to repurpose buildings or rooms designed with an inward intent—a family recreation center, for example. As churches transition to gospel-centrality, they wonder what to do with big buildings designed to keep their church folks isolated from the world. What do you do with an auditorium?

There are no easy answers to these questions, but when I do church consulting, my typical answer is to repurpose it. Can it be used to host the neighborhood? To feed the hungry? Can the recreation area be open to anybody in the community? Could it be leveraged toward sharing the gospel? How can you turn it into an arena of service?

The same concept applies to programs started to facilitate more fellowship within the church, which end up keeping congregants from spending time with their neighbors. If a program cannot be cut—and most should be—can it be repurposed? Can the ladies' tea have an open door to host ladies who don't belong to the church? Can you invite guest speakers who may be of interest to people asking questions about the faith?

Commission Community Groups

Some churches now call their small groups "missional communities" because they see the community as a means of representing Christ to their unbelieving neighbors. This is fine and good.

Not all groups need to function this way, but more of them probably should. It is healthy for a church to have multiple forms of community groups, so long as the groups maintain a study of God's Word and a confessional authenticity with each other. More groups should be open to hosting unbelievers, and more groups should be open to an occasional service or evangelistic mission.

Plant Churches

The most effective means of reaching cities and communities with the gospel is to plant a new church. It's not the only way to reach them, but it's frequently the most impactful. While there is nothing biblically wrong about the multisite model, planting of new churches is a better alternative to launching satellite campuses. The ideal way to facilitate growth is not to start more services, build new sanctuaries, or establish more video venues, but to plant new churches.

One way to remain attractional—guided by pragmatic and con-sumeristic concerns—is to turn the missional mandate we've talked about in this chapter into a "feature" of your church, just one more program people can opt out of. But this is fundamentally different from becoming a missional church centered on the gospel. Pastor J. R. Briggs writes,

> Prioritizing sending capacity over seating capacity isn't a small tweak or a new paint job; it doesn't entail a few programmatic changes to the church calendar. No, it means cultivating a new ethos, shifting the paradigm and changing the posture of the community, which ultimately shapes everything the church is and does.[5]

Over time, the gospel preached, applied, and empowered by the Spirit will coalesce a church around Christ, and from this gospel focus, people can be galvanized to move outward in mission. Consider the difference between centripetal force and centrifugal force, for example. An excellently run attractional church has centripetal force, ever drawing people to the center. A gospel-centered missional church has centrifugal force, where people brought into orbit around the gospel are sent out into the world on mission in response to the explosively glorious power of grace.

Turning Inside Out

"You're about to turn the church upside down," Sandy said.

"More like right-side up, I hope," Josh replied. "And I hope we will be able to do it together."

Drake smirked. "You're making my dreams come true, boss."

"Well, in that case, I ought to rethink the whole thing!"

"Ha. You know I'm with you. I don't know how much my support will matter with some people, but I'm excited about the future. What you're really doing is turning the church inside out."

Josh lit up. "Yes. That's it. We've been turned inward all this time, despite our image of ourselves as being for outsiders. It's time we help people grow and grow more outward."

Sandy brought them both back to earth. "The kind of radical change you're talking about here is likely to send a lot of people out in more ways than one."

CHAPTER 9

The Three Things You Will Need

Your model is only as strong as your mentality

I don't think I can do this anymore."

This time it wasn't Josh talking about his years of attractional ministry. It was Matt, LifePoint's creative arts director. He could see the changes coming. Josh and Rob hadn't implemented too much yet, but the worship service was changing first. The shift seemed imminent. And it directly affected his role.

"I just don't get it," he said.

"What don't you get?" Josh asked.

"I don't really get the purpose. But I also don't get why we need to change anything. Who does that? Churches that are dying. Not churches like ours. You don't get to thousands of people and blow everything up."

"I'm not blowing everything up," Josh said.

"Reboot. Whatever you call it. It's not innovation. It's re-creation."

"Yes, you're exactly right. We're resetting everything."

"Why?"

"Because the way we've done ministry isn't as biblical as it could be."

"I wish you'd quit saying *we*. Maybe you mean *you*. *I* don't think our way is unbiblical. You do. *We* didn't decide this. You did."

This was the first argument Matt and Josh had ever had. For so long they had been on the same page, working in complementary tandem. Maybe that's why Matt was so upset. He felt ambushed by Josh's conviction, like Josh had changed the rules suddenly.

"I wasn't hired to do this," he said.

Now Josh was beginning to lose his patience. "You were hired to serve the church and help me."

"Which I agreed to do based on the vision you cast."

"The vision has changed, Matt."

"No kidding."

"What is it, specifically, that you don't like?"

"A lot of stuff. I don't like the songs. They're weird. I don't like the time it will take to reteach them to people who also think they're weird. I don't like having less freedom creatively. The whole reason I loved LifePoint was because of the creativity."

Josh said, "Think about that, Matt. Think about what you're saying. The whole reason you love LifePoint was because of creativity. Not the people. Not the gospel. Not the mission."

"You know what I mean."

"Is it just a place for you to be a performer?"

Matt looked crushed. Josh had taken it too far.

"How can you say that to me? We've sat at this table for several years now, week after week, working on series together. You've applauded everything we've done. I've only ever known you as a supporter and teammate. We thought the same things. And now to you I'm just some wannabe rock star or something?"

Josh could sense this was already out of hand. He had made it worse. Matt was hurt, and there was no reason to heap more hurt on top of that, even if Matt was saying hurtful things himself.

"Matt, I'm sorry. I really am. I wish I could put it all back in my head and pretend I don't feel convicted about this, but I can't. At this stage, I'm more convinced than ever that not going this direction would be disobedience."

"No matter what it costs?"

"Yes," Josh said, but it sounded like he only barely believed it. "No matter what it costs."

Matt's eyes narrowed. He wasn't calmed. He was angrier than ever. Coolly he said, "And all because you decided to have some midlife ministry crisis."

The Making of a Gospel-Centered Change Agent

Pastoral ministry is not for the faint of heart, no matter what kind of ministry. But if you find yourself, as a pastor or church leader, leading a significant transition in your church, you will need to be tenacious and have the mettle to persevere. I am in awe of those who do the work of church revitalization. They walk into declining or dying churches and must often endure pitiful finances, critical congregants, toxic leaders, apathetic neighborhoods, political complexity, institutional rigidity, and spiritual warfare— all in the desperate hope the church will turn around. It often doesn't.

Everyone wants to grow. Nobody really wants to change. And you cannot grow and not be changed by the process. This is why many leaders of church transitions fail and sputter out. It may be that there's nothing wrong with the program or model they want the church to adopt. It may be, more likely, that the leaders aren't able to navigate the difficulties and complexities of the change.

The right model with the wrong leaders is the wrong model.

To lead a transition as significant and culture-shifting as the one from attractional to gospel-centered, you must be significantly discerning and spiritually strong. You may have a lot of skills in your ministry toolkit. You may have read all the relevant books and attended the right conferences. You may be a smart person, a "people person," a savvy manager, and all the rest, but the change will ultimately fail if you are not the right person for the work.

Your model is only as strong as your mentality.

What do you need then?

To effectively make the shift from attractional to gospel-centered, leaders will at least need conviction, courage, and commitment.

Conviction

To lead a transition to become a gospel-centered church you will need conviction, a settled conviction that gospel-centrality is right and is the best thing biblically, ecclesiologically, culturally, and missionally. Gospel-centrality cannot be just another church style or approach. It cannot be a program you're willing to try. It cannot be the latest in a pattern of church-growth techniques you're interested in applying because the last two or three either haven't worked or got boring.

If you don't believe it, it won't work.

This doesn't mean that the power of the gospel is contingent on you. It doesn't mean that gospel-centrality is weak. It simply means that God has designed churches to be led. And a change as big as this one requires leaders who know what they're talking about.

In the story of LifePoint Church, Pastor Josh has had a significant problem from the beginning when he first sensed that something was "off"—his inability to properly articulate the issue. You have probably been just as frustrated in reading about it as the people around him seem to be. Some people could figure it out, but they were already leaning that way themselves. Others had trouble understanding, or seemed unable or unwilling to understand, in part because he couldn't say exactly what *it* was.

The inability to articulate is a common tendency for those moving from attractional to gospel-centered. The paradigm shift is drastic, and the leader is often new to the concept, so as exciting and right as gospel-centeredness appears to be, leaders often neglect to spend adequate time letting their churches come to grips with the philosophy and end up leaving their congregations feeling left behind. Preparing for the transition means preparing personally and philosophically. Read a lot. Listen a lot. Take notes. Write about it in your journal to start working how you articulate this, striving for clarity. Talk it over with people further along than you so they can refine your thinking, strengthen your arguments, poke holes in your misunderstandings, and expand your applications. Gospel-centrality is not simply *a* way of doing church but *the* way of doing church—if you don't share that conviction, you will never have a gospel-driven church. At best, you'll have a gospel-augmented church. You must believe that the principles of gospel-centrality are God's design for people, churches, and ministries, not just the latest wave in church methodology.

Once upon a time, I led the young adult ministry in an attractional megachurch I attended for almost ten years. A friend of mine who worked in the church's arts department started the ministry. He was burdened by the lack of community and discipleship within the college students and twenty-somethings in our church. So he started recruiting leaders. He reached out to the people he knew in the church who could contribute to a successful ministry. In a way, he was assembling his "dream team" for the ministry leadership. Because my friend is a people-loving, collaboration-loving, creativity-loving person with a huge heart, he brought in a sizable group of leaders. I happened to be one of them, and while most of the team had creative-type gifts, I was "the teaching guy."

You can probably sense where this is going.

My friend knew that I knew the Bible pretty well and was able to teach. He didn't ask me about ministry philosophy or message trajectory. In the beginning, the idea was that we'd all get together and hash out what the group was going to be.

As you should know by now, the message changes the movement.

I started ruffling feathers right away, not because I was mean or a jerk to anybody. I hate conflict and will usually do anything I can to avoid it. My sinful tendencies lean more toward timidity and cowardice than contentiousness. Rather, the frustration came because I was utterly convinced that the ministry should be centered on the gospel, which ruled out some other options. And since I would be doing the teaching, I also believed this teaching would establish the ministry philosophy of the group. (Actually, it's more accurate to say that the ministry philosophy establishes the teaching.)

Some folks were saying the worship service we conducted could be anything we wanted it to be; the whole thing was a blank canvas. We could have pottery wheels and painting stations. We could do whatever music we wanted.

I was the nerdy guy in the circle saying, "If that's what it's going to be, I can't be a part of it." That kind of shut the whole thing down because I was the only teacher. It looked like I was blackmailing everybody. I knew it did. But I didn't know what else to do. I couldn't in good conscience participate in free-for-all worship with an ambiguous purpose. If that's what everybody wanted, I was willing to step down. But our recruiting friend wanted teaching. So stepping down would have killed the whole thing.

It was in a few of those group meetings where I was really pressed inwardly to determine what I really believed. Was I just being stubborn? Or did I actually believe the gospel of Jesus must drive all we do? Was I being a theological egghead? Or did I actually believe that gospel-centered preaching and teaching was the biblically ordained model for transformation?

I'd never seen it done before. I wasn't raised in church environments that discipled me into that. But what I did have was an encounter with the Lord in the midst of a deep depression. I did have God's rescuing hand grab hold of my heart in the darkness of a guest bedroom. I was never the same after that. I had the Bible, which began to shape my thinking on the church and worship in more profound and intensive ways. I was drawing more of my ideas from God's Word than from the world. And I found I couldn't think about ministry the same way anymore.

As I tried to articulate it in those early days, I struggled. Doubtless that is why many on the team couldn't understand what I was talking about. The problem wasn't entirely with them, but with me and my inability to communicate the importance of gospel-centrality with definition, simplicity, and conviction. But a few sort of caught my drift. They were intrigued. They wanted in. The rest tagged along, but I know it was a struggle for them because the ministry expression didn't meet their expectations. It wasn't "free" enough.

Eventually we found ourselves at loggerheads. A new member had been added by our friend, and he was the most vocal critic I had. He wasn't mean. Just consistently contrasting, to the point of being annoying. We had a big team meeting where I tried articulating again what my vision for the ministry was. (At this point I should also tell you that the senior pastor of our church, who was new to our church himself, was not a lot of help, mainly because he didn't understand what I was doing either. I mean, *I* didn't totally understand it then myself.) This new member pressed hard. "Why are we doing it this way? Just because you say? Why do you get to decide?" The implication was that the teaching was just one element of the service, equally weighted with everything else, and thus I shouldn't have so much directional influence on the ministry.

To make matters more complicated, the ministry wasn't growing the way student ministries in attractional environments are expected to. Surely this was proof that my way didn't work. I wish I could say I convinced everyone in that meeting that gospel-centrality was the greatest thing since sliced bread—since *before* sliced bread! I didn't. Our team split roughly in half, with one side dropping out of the ministry and the other side sticking with the philosophy I was demonstrating better than I was articulating.

Our vision for a gospel-centered, missional ministry to young adults became a church within an attractional church. Nobody wanted that, including me. So I met with a few elders and told them I wanted to "take" the ministry and plant it as a new church. They didn't get it, but in their graciousness and goodness, they gave the happy okay and wished us well.

My convictions were put to the test even more. It was somewhat easier when somebody else was paying the bills. Now we were on our own. I got better at articulating the philosophy, and we got better at execution. But we had no one showing us how to do it. There were no local models of gospel-centered, missional church planting. The Acts 29 church planting network wasn't in Nashville yet. A few large churches had elements we liked, but there was nobody we could follow. We had to wing it with the Spirit's help.

The church did not grow. To their wonderful credit, none of my team ever said, "We shouldn't be doing this. It doesn't work." I think

I know why. It wasn't simply that they were gospel-centered people. They were, but that wasn't it. At that point, they still hadn't entirely figured out what gospel-centrality means. (A few of them have since far surpassed me.) No, I think they were "in" because they knew I was. They could tell I bought this stuff. I wasn't going to be dissuaded by low attendance, even if I was disappointed or discouraged by it. They knew I wasn't going to switch up my style. I talked about the gospel being the center *as if I really believed it.*

Your model is only as strong as your mentality.

Of the gospel and gospel ministry, Martin Luther wrote in his commentary on Galatians, "Most necessary it is, therefore, that we should know this article well, teach it unto others, and beat it into their heads continually."[1] Beating it into people's heads isn't meant to be literal; it speaks to the need to combat the average Christian's gospel amnesia. As Luther knew, before pastors can do gospel-centered ministry, they must be gospel-centered personally. "Most necessary it is, therefore, that we should know this article *well.*"

Is "gospel-centered" merely your current preoccupation? Or is it your conscience and conviction? You'll need that conviction to see it through, especially when people question, complain, argue, challenge, accuse, gossip, divide, disrupt, and leave.

And you'll also need courage.

Courage

Being utterly convinced of gospel-centrality is a great start, but it's not enough. You must also have strength in your convictions, the courage to act upon them. People may be angry. People may simply be lazy or apathetic. People may even leave. To make the grace-shift, leaders will need courage to trust this is God's good design.

After a couple of years pastoring that church plant, my wife and I followed God's call to New England. I went from trying to lead a brand-new church plant in suburban Nashville to trying to lead a two-hundred-year-old church in rural Vermont. The experts would say I needed a different model. If by this they mean a different "style," then sure. You don't do the exact same things culturally in rural Vermont, especially with a significantly older congregation, as you might in Nashville with a collection of young adults. The style of music was different. The pacing of everyday life was different. My illustrations were different. The structures and programs we used to apply the gospel organizationally were (a little) different. I didn't preach barefoot like I had in Nashville.

But my conviction was the same. I didn't change my model for a different audience.

I had a couple of people suggest that if I couldn't grow a church in the Bible Belt doing "this gospel stuff," it surely wouldn't work in irreligious New England. I kindly suggested that I was not overly interested in "what worked" but in doing what brought the most glory to Christ and the most transformation to people. I did not change my ministry philosophy or my convictions about preaching. By all common-sense expectations, it should have gone *worse* than it did in Nashville. Instead, our church nearly tripled in size in a few short years. I wasn't even trying to do it. It just happened.

That reminds me of another great Luther quote:

> All I have done is to put forth, preach and write the Word of God, and apart from this I have done nothing. While I have been sleeping, or drinking Wittenberg beer with my friend Philip and with Amsdorf, it is the word that has done great things.... I have done nothing; the word has done and achieved everything.[2]

Granted, it was not without its own challenges. Some people didn't understand why I didn't emphasize more points of application, give them more things to do. By this point, I had a better understanding of what it meant to have a gospel-centered approach to teaching, so I could better articulate it. Some still couldn't quite see it. You may have already discovered that many people don't know what to do with a church that isn't constantly giving them busywork. On the surface, this manifests as a desire to be useful, but in a roundabout way, it can be a not-so-subtle way of having our self-righteousness affirmed.

There were minimal conflicts inside the church as I led them into an embrace of gospel-centrality, away from a traditionalist model of church. But it was wearisome at times. I grew tired trying to apply the gospel. The people seemed to like the preaching, but when I suggested things like throwing a block party for our town on the church lawn, I could see the wheels turning. I was pushing them outward, to engage in ways they'd never been pushed before. I introduced short-term mission trips, thinking that these trips would be more valuable (for us and for our destination partners) if we partnered long-term with the local churches in those areas, financially supporting them throughout the year and returning to the same place every year. I began to cast a vision for a church plant in the "big city" next door. That one really freaked some people out. It took a lot of patient pressing at first, but eventually more than a few came along.

Among other pastors and churches, I felt like a foreigner in a foreign land. I would attend the local evangelical pastors group, a tight-knit gathering, given the occasional hostility to religious institutions in our communities. I saw more interdenominational cooperation in Vermont than I've ever seen anywhere. Christians have to stick together there. But whenever the subject would turn to the question of leading a church, growing a church, or the topic of preaching, I felt like the odd man out. Occasionally I experienced some camaraderie with a youth pastor from another church or an associate pastor. Everybody was very nice to this newcomer, but I hardly ever felt a sense of kinship with another guy in the lead pastor role. I assume it's because we just did things differently. A few older pastors kindly suggested I was still too young to know what they knew and that I would probably grow out of whatever it was I thought I was doing.

I don't share any of this to complain. I share it because I understand. I had ample opportunities to give up on the whole thing. It would have been a lot easier to just give people what they want.

You may find yourself in situations like this, or worse.

I only know a small handful of pastors of megachurches who have attempted transitioning their church in the way I've described in this book, toward greater gospel-centrality. There's a reason for that. *It's freaking hard.* (Note to my editors: Don't put that on the back cover of the book. Nobody will want to read it.) The few who have done this share a settled conviction that gospel-centrality is more biblical and fruitful than attractional ministry, and they also possess an incredible amount of courage, fueled by the Holy Spirit and the grace of Christ, to endure the threat of losing everything.

One friend of mine has lost hundreds of people to a transition in this direction, despite moving slowly, patiently, strategically, and incrementally. He changed the rules, and he's not only lost attendees, but some of the confidence of those who stayed. The people who remain are loyal, but they're confused and sad, because the church appears to be declining. He's had to cut staff and programs due to the financial constraints of losing people. His church is still large compared to most churches, but not as large as it was before he decided to stop protecting "success" from the gospel.

You should know that no matter how slowly and patiently you move, no matter how well and how often you articulate the reasons for the transition, and no matter how great a preacher and savvy a leader you are, this magnitude of transition will bring conflict. Change almost always does. The authors of *Leading Congregational Change* write,

> In our pilot project with . . . congregations, we had assumed that they had the resources needed to manage conflict. In fact, it became clear that one of the prevailing assumptions . . . was that a healthy congregation did not have conflict. As one pastor said, "All my life, I've judged my success by how happy everyone in the church was. You are telling me that if I'm really on mission with God, one sign of my success will be the presence of conflict."[3]

Yes. Remember that counterfeits and warfare are "signs" Jonathan Edwards suggests don't *disprove* a genuine move of God. Edwards reasons that wherever God is really moving, we should expect Satan would be actively trying to sabotage.

Apart from that, there is the typical confusion and conflict that comes from the disruption. People who misunderstand or who feel misunderstood often express criticism in church environments because church is a place where they expect to feel comfortable. They expect to feel like they belong. When significant change happens, it can disrupt their sense of participation. They're not mad at you; they're just hurt from the discomfort of the change.

You can also make people angry by making the gospel central. People whose hearts are tuned to consumerism, self-help moralism, feel-good worship, know-nothing community, or do-nothing mission get upset when the gospel compels repentance. They will get *really* upset when you suggest that the things they've always loved either aren't necessary or may be harmful to them.

You discover a church's idols by changing things.

People will leave. Programs will stop. Giving will drop. Gossips will divide. Activists will undermine. Staff will revolt.

You will be courageous.

How do I know? Because you've committed.

Commitment

Leaders need the conviction and courage to see the transition through to the end. Gospel-driven leaders have a stick-to-itiveness! It doesn't mean you get it all right. It doesn't mean you don't fail. It doesn't mean you don't get tired or discouraged or upset. But it does mean you don't give up. When one more phone call is about to send you over the edge, when one more staff member threatens to quit, when three more families move on to the church down the road with the sense enough to know that kids need entertainment, when the guys in the network or in the local association or in the denominational headquarters think you're a lunatic—don't give up.

My ministry theme verse will forever be 1 Corinthians 2:2. Here it is (emphasized) within its immediate context:

> When I came to you, brothers and sisters, announcing the mystery of God to you, I did not come with brilliance of speech or wisdom. *I decided to know nothing among you except Jesus Christ and him crucified.* I came to you in weakness, in fear, and in much trembling. My speech and my preaching were not with persuasive words of wisdom but with a demonstration of the Spirit's power, so that your faith might not be based on human wisdom but on God's power. (2:1–5 CSB)

The NIV says, "I *resolved* to know nothing while I was with you except Jesus Christ and him crucified" (emphasis added). I like that: *resolved*.

The most serious problem in the Corinthian church at the time of Paul's writing is the worldliness creeping into their mix. The Corinthian converts had not adequately separated their new, Christian ways of living and thinking from their old lives as immoral pagans. Consequently, their spirituality, and their sense of Christianity itself, had been infected by the appetites of their former and allegedly abandoned identities as unbelievers.

Today too many churches believe that we can reach the world with the message of Christ by appealing to people with the things of the world, with spectacle, showmanship, and production. Paul never thinks to do this. He never suggests that more of what you left behind is the best route to what lies ahead. You don't win godly saints in worldly ways. You don't turn sinners into saints with a worldly message.

Paul says, "I did not come with brilliance of speech or wisdom" (v. 1 CSB).

He's not saying brilliance or wisdom aren't good; he's simply saying that's not what he came trusting in. He didn't make them the hallmark of his ministry. Why would anyone do that? Well, you would do that if you think the gospel needs some help.

The question before us today is this: How much weight can the gospel carry?

Is the gospel powerful enough to see you through?

To be a gospel-driven agent of change, you will need the conviction, the courage, and the commitment to see the process through, whether that's simply more gospel-centrality in your church or as drastic as your job security being put to a vote.

Will you resolve to know nothing among them but Christ and him crucified?

As Paul might say, "I am not moving on from this message! I am not departing from this message! You may depart from it around me, but this is the message. I am not moving." Leader after leader, religious consumer after consumer, may come to you with a laundry list of reasons why you should abandon this post.

"Shouldn't you be more creative?" No, this is nonnegotiable.

"You should talk more about politics." No, this is nonnegotiable.

"Why aren't you being more applicational?" This is nonnegotiable.

"Not every text is about Jesus." No, the whole Bible is about Jesus. This is nonnegotiable.

If you devote yourself to the centrality of the gospel, you will confuse and sometimes lose even Christians from your ministry trajectory. Our flesh yearns for more. But we must, with laser-like focus, fix our eyes on the gracious Christ. He is the author and perfecter of our faith, and we must resolve to know nothing except for Christ and him crucified.

D. A. Carson has suggested that one generation assumes the gospel, the next generation loses the gospel, and the next generation must recover it.[4] In 2017 we commemorated the 500th anniversary of the Reformation, the greatest gospel recovery movement in church history, sparked when Martin Luther is said to have nailed his Ninety-Five Theses to the church door in Wittenberg. Thesis sixty-two reads: "The true treasure of the church is the most holy gospel of the glory and grace of God."

Is it your true treasure? Enough to sell every ministerial bell and whistle you've got in order to "own" it? For Luther, it was important enough to deface church property, risk death, and in the face of inquisition to say, in so many words, "Here I stand, I can do no other. So help me God."

We are on the precipice of yet another gospel recovery movement.

We are looking down the exhaust of a generation of church ministry that tried to win the world to Jesus in worldly ways and lost the gospel of Jesus along the way. What we need are ministers willing to resolve—in the face of criticism and pragmatic ministerial wisdom, in a noisy culture of church-growth strategies, religious technology, visionary dreaming, clever programming, attractional maneuvering—to know nothing but Christ and him crucified.

May a new generation of ministers say, "Here we stand. We will do no other."

No matter how stormy the seas get, we will lash ourselves to the mast of the gospel.

Are you with me?

LifePoint Rebooted

"Bob, are you with me?"

Another couple of months had passed, and Josh was about to head into the biggest vision meeting with his leaders yet. All the key staff and directors, as well as all the team leaders, would be in attendance. It would be the first time some of them would hear from him what exactly was going on. It was time to lay out the plan.

At the moment, however, he was hosting Bob Root, LifePoint's pastor for care, in his office. Bob had seemingly wandered in just to make chit-chat, something Bob was very frequently given to do. The joke around the pastoral team was that Bob didn't actually work. The truth is, Bob was the minister with the least amount of administrative duties and the most amount of personal care encounters. In that regard, he worked harder than them all.

Today, though, Josh sensed something was up. Bob knew the meeting was imminent, and it wasn't like him to even tempt a distraction of focus beforehand. Josh sensed Bob was nervous about something, though he'd never come out and say it.

Bob repeated the question like he was asking it to himself. "Am I with you?"

"Yes. The reboot."

"Ah, the plan."

"Yes, Bob. The plan."

"Oh, you know I'm always with you. Whatever you're doing, that's the thing to do."

"Well, I appreciate your loyalty there, but I really want to know if I can count on you to support it, help implement it. I know you won't rock the boat. I want to know if you'll help us row."

Bob sighed. Josh knew that in Bob's heart, he honestly didn't care. He wasn't upset about anything, he wasn't against anything, he wasn't going to criticize or undermine or passive-aggressively patronize. He was just . . . Bob. The guy who goes along.

But Josh also knew that the higher and more invested a leader was in the church, the more impact not buying-in would have. If Bob were simply a guy working the parking team or greeting people at the front door, it would be important if he understood the importance of gospel-centrality and could articulate it well, but it wouldn't seriously hinder the ministry if it took some time. For a pastor, however, he really needed Bob to be there.

"Have I ever gone against you?" Bob asked. He seemed hurt.

"No, you haven't. And it would have been okay, I think, if you had, because I know your heart. You and I have been here the longest. You were here when Dave and Mike were the hotshots, and you always encouraged me. I don't know if I've been helped by any pastor in my life more than I've been helped by you. And so, I want you to know I'm not trying to pressure you or push you or get you to agree with something you don't agree with. It actually makes me really uncomfortable to press you on this. But the changes coming to LifePoint are significant. They're not the kind of things I think we can just tolerate. At our level—yours and mine, as pastors—we have to embrace this, or it won't work."

"Something would have to give," Bob said.

"Basically, yes. I wish that wasn't the case, but I think it is. Something would have to give."

Bob looked like he might cry, though Josh had never seen him do so. He was always so . . . well, Bob. "Even if what has to give is me?"

Josh summoned up his courage and said as gently, as tenderly, as pastorally as he could, "I really hope it doesn't come to that, man. I love you. But, yes, this is more important than any of us. Including me."

The older man seemed to appreciate the honesty. "Well, there it is, then," he said.

Time was ticking. People would be gathering already in the auditorium for the presentation.

"Can we talk about this after the meeting?" Josh asked. "I don't want to rush whatever it is we need to talk about."

"Oh, sure," Bob said. "Not a problem."

As Josh walked to the auditorium, iPad under his arm, he carried with him the sense of sadness that only comes with a loss. He knew the matter with Bob wasn't settled, but he had to share some other bad news with the team today before his presentation, and the prospect of the whole thing was giving him second thoughts.

Approaching the entrance to the children's wing, he quickly diverted into the hallway and entered the first room on the left, which happened to be a nursing mother's room. Sitting down in a wooden rocking chair, he put his iPad on the floor, folded over onto his knees and prayed.

He had been praying for about five or six minutes when he could begin to hear smatterings of people making their way by the hall to the children's area and toward the auditorium. He couldn't delay any longer. Having summoned up enough weakness to ask God for strength, he arose and walked.

Two minutes later he was standing on the stage. The tech nerds had synced his iPad with the overhead screens, and he brought up the title page of his presentation: "LifePoint Rebooted."

"Hey, folks," he said, addressing the entire team in the seats below him, "we have some really exciting things to talk about today, some things I know you've been hearing about behind the scenes for a few months. Some of you are more aware than others, and rather than cause a lot more confusion and delay implementation much longer, it became time to get everything in front of you, so we can all get on the same page.

"But first, I do have some big news to share with you that I know will upset you. Matt Wright has officially stepped down as creative arts director. Matt has worked with us for a while now, and he's brought nothing but excellence and brilliance to his role. But he has expressed his desire to move on to other opportunities, and we've both agreed that would be the best fit for him and his family. We want to wish him well and bless him. I wish he could've been here today, but he's actually taken a couple of weeks off to visit some family and even inquire about some ministry opportunities closer to his home state, so we'll get a chance to love on him and say some sad goodbyes once he's back."

Josh let that sink in for a bit. Most of the leaders already knew of this development, but only a few knew of the conflict at the center of it. For others, however, this was sudden news, and the little murmurings of crosstalk began, stirring up an undulating din over the front of the auditorium.

Eventually Josh decided it was time to move on.

"All right, guys, thanks for coming, thanks for listening. If you have any questions about that, please feel free to talk to your team leaders or one of the pastors. For the next few weeks, Ryan Chaffin will be leading worship for us, in case anybody was wondering about that.

"Now, as I said, I'd like to roll out some pretty important changes coming to LifePoint. We are calling it, as you can see, LifePoint Rebooted."

Josh proceeded then to lay out the rough sketch of a timeline for changes, taking time at each point to elaborate and clarify. He knew that for almost everyone, this was entirely new. Both the changes and the concepts were new. So he went as slowly as he could.

The further down the timeline Josh described, the less certain he could be about the timing or procedure. The last item on the timeline was leadership restructure, which he was appropriately vague about. He hinted optimistically at reorganizing the leadership teams, pastoral team, community groups, and membership process to ensure LifePointers had more interaction with leaders and more pastoral care in their lives.

The first item on the timeline was the worship service reset. This would be the soonest change, and indeed quite a few things had already changed in the service, though it largely functioned in the same way with the same order. People had noticed Josh's preaching had shifted. They also noticed a few new songs.

Josh spent the most time on this point not simply because it was the nearest milestone they hoped to reach but also because it was the clearest in his mind and because everything else flowed directly from the gospel conviction demonstrated in the weekend worship service.

As he explained the importance of focusing on Jesus, making the gospel "visible" in every sermon and in the worship service as a whole, he could see different heads nodding. People seemed to be tracking. They'd noticed slight changes, and now he was giving meaning to them, "showing his cards." The reception, at least visibly, was appreciative.

But there was Bob on the front row, sitting by himself. He was looking at Josh, but his face was blank. Neither sad nor happy.

In the midst of casting an exciting vision, Josh had a vision of making an announcement at the next meeting about his old friend, and his heart sunk.

CHAPTER 10

Leading Change in a Gracious Way

How to do all this without blowing up your church

M an, you're not even gone, and I already miss you."

"Yeah?"

Josh and Matt were riding in Matt's car down to some hipster coffee shop Matt really liked. It might be the last time he could go there.

He'd been gone for two weeks and had already received multiple offers for worship leader roles. His wife and kids had stayed back with her parents while he returned to tidy stuff up and get things ready for the movers. They would decide on one of the offers in the next two weeks, and then he'd be gone.

The two friends hadn't talked since Matt had put in his resignation, unless a short text exchange about when Matt might be back in town was considered talking. Matt recommended his buddy Ryan, who played guitar in the worship band, to replace him as leader in the interim. That was his way of helping out while getting out.

The conversation so far had been awkward. It was like they'd just put a bandage over the raw nerves exposed in their argument and now they were slowly pulling it off together.

Matt said, "I'm gonna miss you too. It was a blast working with you. Sometimes I step out of my office and walk around and think,

'Man, look at what God did.' It's pretty cool and pretty amazing when you stop to think about it."

"It definitely is," Josh said.

More silence.

Finally Josh ventured: "Look, I don't want to make this weirder than it already is. And thank you, first of all, for inviting me to coffee. I know this is one of your favorite places, and letting your dorky pastor come with you has to lessen the fun of it somewhat."

Matt smiled.

"But," Josh continued, "I just want to say I'm really, really sorry for the way I spoke to you. It wasn't right. It wasn't fair. You mean too much to me and to the church for me to have talked to you in such disrespectful ways. Please forgive me."

Immediately Josh felt he should have waited until they got to the coffee shop to make his apology, because it felt strange to offer it to a guy who was navigating the busy traffic on the interstate. To his relief, however, Matt replied, "Man, I'm sorry too. I was a jerk. I honestly still don't know what the heck you're doing, but I'd be a hypocrite if I expected you not to explore whatever God is calling you to do."

"It's okay," said Josh. "I pushed you. I put you in that position. And honestly, I changed the game on you. I couldn't help it, not really. I hope you know that, but I can totally see how it would come across. We had an agreement, in a way. We had an agreement about how the ministry should go. And I basically reneged."

This seemed to help. Josh halfway expected a "That's right!" triumphalism from Matt, but he didn't get it. Instead Matt actually seemed comforted, happier. If Josh had to guess, he would think that Matt, probably for the first time since the transition, felt like he was halfway understood.

Deep down, most people just want to be understood. A lot of us, of course, just want to be agreed with! But I think most of us just want to be *heard*. Heard and understood.

Gospel-Driven Pastoral Ministry

If you want a gospel-driven ministry, you must resign your will to the supremacy of the glory of Christ and trade your personal ambitions for the beauty of Christ's bride.

Ponder deeply what Paul writes in 1 Corinthians 3:5–9:

> What then is Apollos? What is Paul? Servants through whom you believed, as the Lord assigned to each. I planted, Apollos watered, but God gave the growth. So neither he who plants nor he who waters is anything, but only God who gives the growth. He who plants and he who waters are one, and each will receive his wages according to his labor. For we are God's fellow workers. You are God's field, God's building.

Apollos was a friend of Paul's. Apollos himself profited from Paul's ministry. We learn elsewhere that even though Apollos was a follower of Jesus, he did not have a very robust view of the gospel at first, not enough to begin missionary work. But Priscila and Aquila discipled him and filled out some of what was lacking in his theology. And apparently, Apollos became a very good preacher. He was a real standout: dynamic, engaging, powerful.

If you were surfing iTunes for preaching podcasts or scanning the radio dial looking for good preaching, and you came across both Paul and Apollos, you would choose Apollos. Paul did not speak with eloquence or words of lofty wisdom. Apollos, however, could crush it, bring it, tear it up.

Paul had come to the Corinthians first, laying the foundation of the gospel. To use his own words here, he "planted the seed." Apollos came next to take up the work Paul began. Apollos became the Corinthians' golden boy, and it was inevitable, then, that the church began playing the comparison game.

Imagine how the division might have begun.

"Well, you know I liked Paul, he was a good guy and all, but he couldn't preach his way out of a paper sack. Apollos is the real deal."

Others might say, "Well Apollos is a good preacher, true, but I'm still loyal to Paul. He's the one who really got us in shape and headed in the right direction."

Then somebody might say, "Paul's always writing here griping about stuff. Apollos never did that. He was always positive."

Or somebody might have said to Apollos, "You know, Paul never did it that way."

Paul knows this is happening and says (in verse 4), "Well, aren't you acting like mere humans?"

Not that they shouldn't be human, of course, but they were acting as reduced persons, as just "merely human." They were making decisions, pledging allegiances, and tuning their hearts all according to appetites and preferences and styles and personalities. Of course, people still do this! The more things change, the more they stay the same.

What's instructive is that Paul did not see Apollos as a threat. Paul was not envious or jealous. Paul saw Apollos as someone gifted by God to spread the fame of Jesus far and wide, and that's what Paul wanted most of all. Whoever best helped the gospel go to the ends of the earth, *that's* who Paul was interested in. Paul was saddened not by Apollos's fame but by the Corinthians' divisiveness because of human speakers.

This is the New Testament's version of the "celebrity preacher" problem. But the issue runs much deeper than consumeristic ecclesiological preferences. It runs straight to the heart—of the sheep and the shepherd. The desire to have more than we're given, to accomplish more than we're assigned, to be more than we are is something that lies just beneath the surface of the fallen heart.

If you want to be driven by the gospel in pastoral ministry, you have to tune your heart to realities deeper than gifts and experiences. These are Spiritual realities about the pastor's identity and the nature of pastoral work. Here are three important ones.

Gospel-Driven Pastors Know What They Are

We have today a long trail of bodies left by ministers of the gospel who have fallen—morally, ethically, spiritually. Names are coming to your mind right now. Maybe you're one of them. These pastors have fallen from the ministry, but they fell long before that, when they got too big for themselves, when they forgot *what they are*.

As Paul wrote in 1 Corinthians 3:5, "What then is Apollos? What is Paul? They are servants through whom you believed, and each has the role the Lord has given" (CSB).

Notice first that Paul doesn't ask, "*Who* is Apollos? *Who* is Paul?"

For one thing, the Corinthians knew *who* these guys were. They know Apollos is the guy headlining all the conferences, that he's the only orthodox guy with a book in the religion section at Target. "We know Apollos. He has seventy thousand Twitter followers."

But Paul's not asking *who*. He's asking *what*.

"What is Apollos? What is Paul?"

That's a different question. *What are you?*

This is *the* question. Many pastors are too keenly aware of *who* they are. They will tell anybody who doesn't seem to know: "Don't you know who I am?"

Okay, maybe you don't say it. But from time to time you may think it. You don't have to be a "big platform" guy with a large-scale ministry to think this way, just a sinner worried about being cheated of honor.

"What then is Apollos? What is Paul? They are servants."

The word here translated "servant" is the Greek word *diakonoi*, the same word that gives us the English word for the church office of deacon.

If you're always grumbling about your deacons, I got news for you: you is them, and they is you! Yes, in office and in governance, you "outrank" them, but in service to the Lord, you are no greater, no less. We are all—whether planters, waterers, or harvesters—servants. We need to remember that servants don't make the food, they just serve it.

We quench the Spirit when we mistake our work for God's work. You can't do what God does. You can only be what you are.

Don't forget what you are: a servant. A waiter. A busser. But it's not enough to remember what you are.

Gospel-Driven Pastors Know What They Are Not

Not only are Paul and Apollos simply servants, busboys in the house of God, they are *nothing*:

> I planted, Apollos watered, but God gave the growth. So then neither the one who plants nor the one who waters *is anything*, but only God who gives the growth. (1 Cor. 3:6–7 CSB, emphasis added)

Compared to the glory of the God who made all things, sustains all things, declares all things, controls all things, these puny apostles and preachers are nothing. Not even dirt, not even a speck of dust swirled up into the eternal cosmos—they are nothing.

Paul in this moment has so abandoned himself to God's sovereignty, waylaid by the grace of God, that Paul feels privileged to be used at all. In the back of Paul's mind has to be the reality that he was not seeking God when he was found. God hijacked *him*. If anybody knew what being subjected to sovereignty meant, it was Paul. He was God's enemy when God enlisted him to proclaim God's glory.

The same Paul who says in 1 Corinthians 9:22, "I have become all things to all people," also says later in 15:9, "I am the least of the apostles, unworthy to be called an apostle."

Paul always saw himself as a fortunate, puny soul in service to the almighty Master and Commander of the universe. From what great love did God make the earth out of nothing, and from what great love has God made the church by the hands of thousands of little "not anythings."

I am reminded of Paul's argument in Galatians that the gospel is better than everybody! He says, even if an angel came and preached to you, if it wasn't the gospel, let that angel be accursed. He says if "I" came to you preaching a different gospel to you, let me be accursed. Why? Because the gospel, he's saying, is bigger than me. It is better than me. And you, Galatians, ought to be centered on the gospel, not on me.

He even takes a poke at the other apostles in Galatians 2:6:

> And from those who seemed to be influential (what they were makes no difference to me; God shows no partiality)—those, I say, who seemed influential added nothing to me.

The gospel is bigger than any pastor.

Do you conduct ministry like *you* are the gospel to your church, as if *you* really make the difference?

We live in a day when the creativity in job titles seems endless. Many of these titles—which, let me just say, are not all bad in and of themselves—are borrowed from the business world and not found in the Word of God: thought leader, agent of change, catalyst.

And all along, I was under the impression that the Holy Spirit was the one working through the gospel as the catalyst for change.

I honestly don't think it matters what you call yourself. But we cannot forget that the power to change comes from the gospel of Jesus Christ.

Apollos? Paul? Just servants. No big whoop. You can always hire more servants. A bus comes buy and wipes out Paul. Hey, there's Apollos. Apollos is out playing nine holes and gets struck by lightning. Well, who else have we got?

Pastors are invaluable, but your gifts, your talent, your strategies, your vision are all expendable.

I hope you see what Paul is doing and why he's doing it. He is so wrapped up in the enormity and the effectiveness and the utter necessity of Jesus Christ, that he and everybody else who would preach Jesus are being shrunk down to mere tools in Jesus's hands.

Pastors aren't the power. The gospel is the power. So pastors driven by the gospel don't forget what they aren't.

Gospel-Driven Pastors Remember What Lasts

I once spoke to a guy from a large church about funding plans for a church plant. He was going through a list of routine questions and asked me, "When was your church started?"

I said, "In the late 1780s."

There was a long pause on the other end of the phone line.

He finally said, "I've never gotten an answer like that before."

"Yeah," I joked. "I'm just the latest warm body."

I had a filing cabinet in my study with the church records to prove it—name after name of faithful ministers, mostly forgotten today. Every now and then a minivan would roll onto the Middletown green, and a few middle-aged folks would knock on our door. They'd want to look at the records for ancestry research. But by and large, what was left of these ministers, members, deacons, and board members was a scribbled name in a crumbling book in a janky file cabinet in a little country church. It was a constant reminder to me that one day *my* name was going to be a barely legible entry in a dusty book covered in mouse droppings.

That provided some clarity about my place in ministry.

Paul writes:

> He who plants and he who waters are one, and each will receive his wages according to his labor. For we are God's fellow workers. You are God's field, God's building. (1 Cor. 3:8–9)

Here Paul was doing something provocative. It would make sense to compare the minister to God and say, "The minister is *nothing* compared to God." But he compares the minister to *what*?

To the church.

Jesus did not promise that the gates of hell would not prevail against your ministry empire. Only the church will prevail.

Your diplomas and certificates and letters of recommendation will be thrown in the grave. What about your best-turned phrases and stylistic eloquence? In the grave. Your blog posts or book deals? In the grave. Your growth strategies and big ideas? In the grave. That sign outside with your name on it? In the grave.

Revelation 4 reminds us that every crown you possess will be thrown at the feet of the only one the grave cannot hold.

And if you would escape the grave, if you would like to see your legacy live on into eternity, you must place your legacy at the feet of Jesus Christ. God is putting all things in subjection under him. And in the end, he will stand triumphant over the field he has tended, the building he has built. Only the church will last.

You're just a worker. The church is God's field, God's building. The church belongs to him, and he will cultivate you, he will build you, he will sustain you, he will empower you, he will nourish you, he will transform you, and he will save you.

"For no one can lay any other foundation than what has been laid down," Paul writes (v. 11 CSB). "That foundation is Jesus Christ."

It is far better to inherit the legacy of Christ than to build a legacy of your own.

When John the Baptist began his prophetic work, he was picking up ministry after four hundred years of silence. There had been four hundred years of God's people not hearing from God, and then John shows up. (And you thought your ministry was super relevant!)

John was not exactly the most likely "catalyst for growth." He wore camel fur and ate bugs—so, you know, *not attractional.* Yet people flocked to his ministry.

Then Jesus showed up. And John, with all his crowds and all his following and all his influence and all his success, says, "I'm not fit to untie his shoes." And "he must increase. I must decrease."

And what does Jesus say about John? In Matthew 11:11, Jesus basically says that John is the greatest guy who ever lived.

Your name may be forgotten on earth in a hundred years, but it is written forever in the Lamb's Book of Life. When Christ comes to reclaim his bride—big, small, planter, or waterer—he will be rejoicing to receive you.

You want success? Pastor Scott Sauls writes:

When God gives us success for a time—when he chooses to put the wind at our backs—by all means, we should enjoy it. But we mustn't hang our hats on it, because earthly success, in all its forms, comes to us as a gift from God and is fleeting. Our Lord is telling us not to allow appetizers to replace the feast, or a single apple to replace the orchard, or a road sign to replace the destination to which it points.[1]

The gospel-driven pastor knows what he is, what he is not, and what ultimately lasts. We are "not anything." Only God is. Let us pastor from that reality.

Ten Keys to Shepherding the Transition

The key word here, before we get into the keys, is *shepherding*. Transition must be shepherded, or pastored, as much as (if not more than) managed. In transitions you get to put the biblical qualifications for the pastorate to the test. The verses in 1 Timothy 3:1–7, Titus 1:5–9, and 1 Peter 5:1–4 remind us of all the heart and character work we might neglect throughout the course of church ministry. We drift into programmatic mode, leaning heavily on our skills, education, and gifts, and forget that our abilities can never replace our character. Leadership skills and administrative aptitude will be advantageous in a church change, but a failure to be peaceable, humble, or slow-tempered will derail even the most skilled ministry manager.

The church needs a team of shepherds, especially during significant transitions, who will feed the flock. After you're sure you're shepherding, here are ten keys to administer a transition in a gracious way.

1. Take It Personally, but Don't Make It Personal

To "take it personally" is simply to make sure you have the gospel conviction discussed in chapter 9. Have you owned the need for change? Do you understand the content that you want to replace pragmatism? Have you thought about the possible outcomes? Is this something you are convicted about doing and committed to seeing through, or is it simply the latest ministry fascination or way to "shake things up"?

Take it personally.

But don't make it personal. In other words, don't tune your ups and downs to how people react, to what ground is lost or made up, to how the service is performing, etc. It is quite possible to make gospel-centrality into an idol. And it is incredibly possible to make an idol of your church specifically or of ministry in general. Putting these two things together is a recipe for spiritual disaster. Do not seek to change your church toward gospel centrality because of your own unresolved issues of works righteousness and personal success. "Without realizing it, leaders can paint their own dysfunction over churches, ministries, and mission fields. All too easily, the effort to preach the gospel becomes about appeasing fears and insecurities, turning leadership into a tool used to primarily gain a sense of personal meaning."[2] Some things are about you, sure. But not even everything that's about you is really about you. Your church has not been stewarded to you in order to make you feel complete or fulfilled as a Christian or a pastor. Only the gospel can do that. Don't treat the church like your emotional support animal, and you won't be as tempted to imagine every conflict, every question, every hiccup as pertaining to you.

2. Practice the Spiritual Fruit of Patience

Give people time to process the transition. Don't rush them. People usually prefer to be led and not pushed. Hold as many hands as you need, not to delay progress but to ward off confusion about the progress.

People understand at different rates. Remember that simply moving forward is walking in obedience. Don't assume you aren't being faithful until you *arrive*.

Remember how patient God was with you before you "got it." Don't treat others who are slow to grasp gospel-centrality with pressure you were not subjected to. People rarely feel leveraged into a genuine comprehension of grace.

Don't pester through the change. Be patient.

3. Move Slowly and Strategically

Forward progress at a snail's pace is not ideal, but it is preferable to going backward because you pushed too hard. Choose your shots. Don't try to change everything at once. Make incremental goals based on the congregation's ability to absorb the change. (See appendix 2 for a suggested prioritization of goals.) Then move as slowly as obedience will allow. Some churches will change fast. Most, especially more established churches, will take more time. Don't bulldoze your way through it.

In an interview with *For the Church* on leading big change in a church without "blowing it up," Pastor Clint Pressley said that leaders must act a little bit like barometers, gauging the congregation's threshold of toleration for change. Pressley says that the pastor must take care to keep the church moving forward, keeping them at the threshold of tolerance without going too far.[3]

4. Show Meekness and Give Mercy

When conflict arises, as it often does during significant change, it is so easy to slip into self-justification mode. Gracious leaders, however, constantly repent of defensiveness and constantly stay on guard against becoming domineering, something Peter specifically forbids pastors from doing (1 Peter 5:3).

One way I have learned to work against handling conflict sinfully is to advocate in my mind for my critics. What if their problem isn't with you but with change? Maybe they're taking out frustrations on you, but it's not really about you. What if they're just uncomfortable? Or confused? Or unaccustomed to managing their feelings in productive ways? Or going through a difficult personal problem that is bubbling over?

Sin is sin, of course, and pastors must address divisive, short-tempered, gossiping, or otherwise quarrelsome members. But a lot of conflict could be prevented if we were slow to speak, quick to listen, and reluctant to engage in unfruitful debates. Forgive people. Give them mercy by not fighting back.

Pastor Ronnie Floyd offers this advice on leadership meekness:

As pastors, we can get into trouble when we choose to die on the wrong hills. When we do this, we lose not just sleep, but also our brand. Our testimony can become questionable among God's people. The greatest leadership lesson I have ever learned is that not every hill is worth dying on. There are definitely hills that we must be willing to die on, hills where we do not give one inch. Some of those include key doctrines like the authority of Scripture, morals that violate Christ's teaching, and ethics that harm our testimony. There are others, but these are some of the bigger hills where we need to stake our flag. Dying on secondary hills is unwise. When you die on every hill, when you have to be right or feel you must have the last word on everything continually, you are setting yourself up to forfeit your leadership.[4]

Embracing meekness keeps us from treating every meeting like a battle, every conversation like a conflict. If you die to yourself, you won't need to die on every hill.

There may be battles to fight, but remember that people are not the enemy. Prepare for spiritual warfare, but don't spiritualize every conflict. Don't make opposite sides of an issue related to transition about "good versus evil." If there's sin, address it, but remember that just because somebody disagrees with you or doesn't understand what you're doing, it doesn't mean they're in sin.

People aren't the devil. They may be influenced by him, but they are not him, and he is not them. Be careful not to think in such hyperspiritual terms that your side becomes the godly side and the other becomes ungodly. There is such a thing as gossip and divisiveness, which are both sins and, according to Scripture, deserving of church discipline. But don't get into the habit of depicting anybody who disagrees with you, even if passionately, as an enemy or a tool of the Enemy. This isn't angels versus demons; it's probably just people on both sides who don't fully understand yet.

Know-it-alls will almost always identify negative reactions to their decisions as the cost of standing for the truth and suffering for the Lord. But leaders may not realize they can wrongly wound people with the right thing. The right thing done the wrong way demonstrates a lack of pastoral wisdom and care.[5]

5. Employ Plurality and Embrace Parity

It's important to present a united front with your fellow leaders. The more leadership is unified in this transition, the less opportunity there is for anyone to say, "Oh, this is just Pastor So-and-So's idea." No, we are following God's idea, and we agree as your pastors that we all want to make sure we adopt it.

In leadership discussions and deliberations, make sure the "first among equals," the lead pastor, isn't just dictating an individual vision. Pursue true parity within levels of leadership. Every qualified pastor ought to have an equal say in how the vision gets implemented, even if there is one "lead" pastor who does most of the communication to the church.

The wider among the church's leadership the vision is applied and the more consensus there seems to be, the more convincing the vision for change will be to the congregation.

6. Overcommunicate

Do not assume that vision-casting is a one and done deal. Communicate what you're doing, where you're going, how you're getting there, and especially why you're doing it, and don't stop. Overcommunicate. Then re-overcommunicate. Then re-overcommunicate again. As Thom Rainer says, "I have never seen or heard a major change initiative and its accompanying vision repeated too much."[6]

What may be compelling and settled in your mind is likely the result of months of deliberation, study, prayer, and collaboration with other leaders. Your congregation has not had that advantage. What will feel old to you will feel brand new to them. Even your enthusiasm may unsettle them at first because as they wrestle through comprehension they will feel the "pressure" of your excitement pushing them to process more quickly than they feel able. The authors of *Leading Congregational Change* write,

> In the excitement to announce the vision and begin implementation, change leaders often forget that the rest of the congregation has not been a part of the intense dialogue and soul-searching that are a part of discerning and articulating the vision. In forgetting this key fact, they underestimate the amount of communication that will be required. To expect commitment from the congregation without adequate interaction and understanding is unrealistic.[7]

I remember leading the annual church budget meeting at my previous church and becoming frustrated at how many questions members had about all the nitty-gritty details of certain line items or budget changes. They wanted to know how we arrived at those numbers. It felt like they were second-guessing or demanding justification for everything. I felt these nitpicky questions amounted to distrust of the leaders elected by the congregation to handle these matters. "If you don't trust them to make sound decisions, don't elect them to the board!" I always wanted to say. What good is it to form a committee to make decisions that you then will rhetorically undermine every year at budget time?

What finally occurred to me was that the folks asking questions simply didn't have the advantage of the time investment enjoyed by leadership. They weren't trying to say that the leadership couldn't be trusted; they were just trying to catch up. Budget committee members had spent months sorting through all the details, praying together to seek God's guidance, and hashing out numbers after asking questions and subjecting themselves to internal critique and scrutiny. The members had mere minutes to take in the resulting information. We should expect that they'd want to slow down a bit and ask for help understanding.

So we started passing out budget proposals a few weeks in advance so people could read them over, seek understanding outside the pressure of an afternoon business meeting, even email questions to committee members. During the meeting, we moved slowly, asking people if they had questions at each stage, trying to make sure anybody willing to raise their hand wouldn't get left behind.

The clear vision in your mind from countless hours of contemplating *for your job* will not be so clear to the congregation, who usually think about it only when you bring it up at church. You need to overcommunicate. When you feel like you've offered too much communication, you're probably just beginning to approach the right amount.

7. Show Your Cards

I hate movies and TV shows that rely on misunderstandings that could've been easily avoided with a simple answered question or a conversation. The '80s TV show *Three's Company* was like that. Every episode, somebody was overhearing one side of a phone conversation and then panicking about what they heard. The episodes would revolve around hijinks related to the misunderstanding. In real life that doesn't happen because we would ask the person we overheard clarifying questions. "Hey, who were you talking to? What was that about?" The same is true in every Hallmark movie when the romantic leads spend ten minutes in crisis toward the end of the movie, right before the romantic reunion, because of a misheard line or misunderstood action. The whole thing could be avoided if they just asked a clarifying question or didn't jump to conclusions.

What they don't say hurts them, and they don't say it because the screenwriter *wants* tension and misunderstanding for the sake of drama and delay. The screenwriter writes lazy characters because misunderstandings advance his or her storytelling. That should never be the case for leaders of gospel change.

Don't be a lazy character in God's story. Don't create tension and misunderstanding when you could create clarity; don't foster drama and delays when you could foster unity. Don't just give the vision, explain it. Clarify why it's important. Demonstrate how you're going to get there. Tell people what it took to arrive at your passion for gospel-centrality. Tell them how long it might take. Tell them what you're worried about, excited about, afraid of, in need of. Show your cards.

8. Operate Consistently

One of the few things more maddening than impotent leadership is inconsistent leadership. Is your willingness to apply the necessary changes in your church erratic? Do you vacillate between excitement and apathy? Does the communication of the vision for gospel-centrality hinge on the times when you're feeling upbeat or "extra gospelly"?

How do you implement change within the congregation? Are you biased toward augmenting or eliminating certain programs? What about transitioning personnel off the team? Do you pick and choose based on easiness or timidity or nepotism?

If so, you're telling people that you're excited for gospel-centrality so long as it's easy to implement. You're communicating that it's not worth having hard conversations about or risking conflict over, that it's not important enough to do the right thing consistently.

Take the example of reducing programs. Maybe you've determined that this change necessitates discontinuing church programs that do not serve the vision. Some pastors will come in and cut the programs that are easiest to cut and let others with stronger or more tender personalities hang around. Why? The pastor doesn't want to hurt anybody's feelings or run afoul of certain power structures in the church. But he's communicating that gospel-centrality isn't worth being consistent about. He's let some people off the hook but not others. And letting people off the hook is actually putting others on it.

Apply gospel-centrality across the board. Doing so might feel like not giving grace to people you're trying to bring in line, but by failing to do this, you are not showing grace to the others who are already in line. You are expecting those who are with you to meet higher standards than the others, and in some cases, you can tempt them into envy or bitterness or even a sense of superiority. The gospel eventually brings justice at every level, including to the teensy-weensy level of church programming, where the old folks want to keep their Sunday School class the way it has always been!

Being consistent brings grace to all parties.

Rainer says, "We don't lead change for change sake. We lead change for the sake of the gospel."[8] This is also true if you, yourself, are always changing. Consistency in seeing gospel-centrality through is key, and it is key to understand that you will never, ever, ever be "through" with gospel-centrality. This isn't a church-growth model; it is God's biblical design for the church, period.

Which isn't to say there aren't other things that change. As cultural challenges shift, as neighborhoods see changes in demographics, as contexts take new forms, the same old message may require new missional wineskins. But the gospel must not be the latest strategy for growth. It must be the only strategy.

9. Cheerlead and Celebrate Wins

It is possible to lead a transition to gospel-centrality in a law-centered way. Doing so will embed an internal defeater in the movement. How can you make sure people don't get burned out on "trying to be gospel-centered"? Create a culture of encouragement. Be your team and your church's lead cheerleader, making a big deal of every success and positive adjustment along the way.

Thank people. Honor people. Bring people into the fold of acknowledgment and celebration. Help them to feel like they belong, that change isn't just happening *to* them but also *by* them.

Don't just be a barometer for change, be a thermostat for optimism, setting the temperature to joy for your church. It's a joyful thing to focus deliberately on Christ and his glory. Go first in that endeavor and set the example.

10. Keep Preaching the Gospel

"Gospel truth lovingly and consistently applied," Ray Ortlund says, "creates a gospel culture." Do not grow faint in this good endeavor.

Don't just overcommunicate the vision for gospel-centrality; overcommunicate the message of the gospel.

Cast and recast the vision of Christ's glory proclaimed in the gospel of his finished work. In the end, you don't simply want the change of a church model; you want the change of the church's heart. The only message that changes hearts is the good news of Jesus's life, death, and resurrection.

As Luther said, "beat it into their heads continually,"[9] only don't be mean about it.

Preach grace and grace alone—and don't give up!—and then watch as the metrics of grace emerge to become the measurement of your church's health over time. Preaching the gospel is the first and most important way to give your church the power it needs to bear fruit for Christ.

A gospel-driven pastor is really the first key to a gospel-driven church.

LifePoint Recentered

Six months later, the reboot of LifePoint was still turning, like a cruise ship reversing course—slowly, in a wide arc. Pastor Josh's preaching was the first thing to change, and at first, people didn't seem to notice. He had finished his series on "Bible heroes," but ended each one showing how the virtues of the heroes of the Old Testament were not enough for their salvation and how Jesus displayed those virtues perfectly. After that he preached a series called "Freedom" that was really an exposition of Ephesians 2. As he emphasized grace more and works less, he did begin to get more emails. He responded kindly, explaining the reason for the shift, why he thought it was important, and what he hoped to accomplish.

Then they publicly announced the reboot. Most people were excited. Some were confused. Nobody was angry, as far as they could tell. Then the music became very different, the "vibe" in the room less produced, and more people left. They cut down to three services, then two. Then Josh began preaching through the book of Galatians. He got a few emails about how they were becoming a "traditional" church. He offered to meet with these folks in person to discuss the changes. Only a few took him up on the offer. Only a few of those stayed at the church.

They eventually had to reduce the number of services. Oddly enough, though their giving did decline, it did not do so significantly, and they didn't need to sort through possible personnel reduction. (Josh had a hunch that the changes were feeding growing Christians, and growing Christians tend to be the most faithful givers.)

He had yet to make some of the bigger changes he and the other pastors felt necessary. A membership overhaul was coming. Working with Rob and Felix, they wanted to basically "zero out" membership and start over, extending the process by which people become members to ensure credible professions of faith and proper pastoral care. That process would also involve an overhaul of their pastor/elder structure. They currently did not have enough pastors to maintain adequate care for members, much less regular attenders seeking help. They were also discussing a new discipleship strategy and small groups structure that would delegate care appropriately and provide plenty of shepherding access without making the pastor/elder team top-heavy in the church.

In the meantime, Josh focused on steering from the stage. Between God-centered music, more biblical content, more prayer during the gathering, and increasingly gospel-centered preaching, he trusted God to be shaping his congregation's heart for the gospel and creating an appetite for more depth and transformation in the community life of the church. Only time would tell if that would happen, but Josh was convinced that if it would, his present trajectory was the only way to get there.

On his way to meet with Ryan, the new worship leader, to discuss upcoming service planning, he caught himself in front of Bob Root's office. The door was open. Bob sat at his desk facing the entryway. A stack of books sat to his right, and he had one open flat in front of him.

Josh had decided to move slowly with Bob. They'd been through a lot together. All the pastors had a lot to learn from him. Bob's attitude about the reboot may not have been ideal for helping to steer the transition, but Josh decided he could work with him for a while, giving him some room. Having known Bob a long time, Josh knew he took a long time to do anything. Making a rash decision on Bob's place in the church would not have been gracious, and it would have been presumptuous and perhaps unhealthy for the church.

"Bob," Josh said. "I didn't know you read books."

He was joking, and Bob knew it. "Well, if they've got enough pictures, I do."

"Whaddya reading, man?"

Bob held up the cover of the open book. "One of your gospelly books."

Josh was legitimately surprised. "Well, all right."

"I figure," Bob said, "sometimes us old guys can learn something new, you know?"

Josh smiled. "Yes sir. I do."

APPENDIX 1

Summary of Principles

Throughout this book I have offered numerous sets of claims, principles, and steps. If you're like me, you may have trouble keeping multiple lists like these straight in your study and reflection time. I've always thought writers and teachers who offer multiple sets of "points" in one volume could help me out by including just a list of the lists, with all the extra stuff cut out. I hope you will find this a helpful reference in reviewing the content of *The Gospel-Driven Church* and perhaps sharing it with others.

The Operating System of the Attractional Church (Ch. 1)

1. Consumerism
2. Pragmatism
3. Legalism/Moralism (Positive Law)

Why Doesn't the Attractional Church Work? (Ch. 1)

1. It is becoming more difficult to think of the model as generationally sustainable.
2. The discipleship culture of the attractional church is ecclesiologically unsustainable.
3. The consumerism of the attractional church wins people not to church but to consumerism.
4. The attractional church is becoming more culturally naïve.
5. The attractional church is evangelistically unsuccessful.

Marks of Neutrality (Ch. 2)

1. A steady accumulation of decisions or responses during Sunday invitations
2. Large attendance
3. Emotional experiences

The Metrics of Grace (Ch. 3)

1. A growing esteem for Jesus Christ
2. A discernible spirit of repentance
3. A dogged devotion to the Word of God
4. An interest in theology and doctrine
5. An evident love for God and neighbor

Reconnecting with Supernatural Christianity (Ch. 4)

1. Recover the supernaturality of prayer.
2. Recover the supernaturality of Scripture.
3. Recover the supernaturality of the gospel.

Why Center on the Gospel? (Ch. 4)

1. The Bible says the gospel is central.
2. The Bible says the gospel is effectual.
3. The Bible says the gospel is versatile.

What is Gospel-Driven Preaching? (Ch. 5)

1. Preaching that proclaims
2. Preaching that exults
3. Preaching that reveals the glory of God in Christ

How Your Worship Service Might Be Upside Down (Ch. 6)

1. Feelings are emphasized before and over doctrine.
2. Lost people are given religious homework.
3. Gospel invitations are offered after a legal message.

Four Irreducible Elements of Gospel-Centered Worship (Ch. 6)

1. Preaching
2. Praying
3. Singing
4. Eating

Why Does Discipleship Matter? (Ch. 7)

1. Discipleship matters because it empowers fidelity to Christ.
2. Discipleship matters because it ensures the witness of the church.
3. Discipleship matters because it expands the glory of God.

Applying the Gospel Organizationally (Ch. 7)

1. Reevaluate polity.
2. Rethink membership.
3. Reorder small groups.
4. Recruit and replicate disciple-makers.

Gospel-Centered, Missional Preaching (Ch. 8)

1. Put the text in the context of God's mission.
2. Make application mission-oriented.
3. Confront idols.
4. Anticipate the right questions.
5. Give the motivation for grace.

Missional Molding (Ch. 8)

1. Specific training
2. Organized opportunities
3. Leadership examples
4. Repurpose programs or structures
5. Commissioned community groups
6. Plant churches

Three Qualities You Need to Lead a Transition to Gospel-Centrality (Ch. 9)

1. Conviction
2. Courage
3. Commitment

The Gospel-Driven Pastoral Ministry (Ch. 10)

1. Pastor from the power of the gospel.
2. Measure yourself from the economy of the gospel.
3. Navigate failure from the justification of the gospel.
4. Measure success from the glory of the gospel.

Ten Keys to Shepherding the Transition (Ch. 10)

1. Take it personally, but don't make it personal.
2. Practice the Spiritual fruit of patience.
3. Move slowly and strategically.
4. Show meekness and give mercy.
5. Employ plurality and embrace parity.
6. Overcommunicate.
7. Show your cards.
8. Operate consistently.
9. Cheerlead and celebrate wins.
10. Keep preaching the gospel.

APPENDIX 2

Gospel-Centered Troubleshooting

The following material will address a variety of applicational and what-if questions that may arise from the positions promoted in this book. Because every context is different, I didn't think it necessary to address every possible contingency or scenario in the chapters, but I still want to explore a few details that may be pertinent in many of your ministries.

The Gospel and Gospel-Centrality

Does preaching style matter in the gospel-centered paradigm?

It depends on what is meant by *preaching style*. There are a variety of temperaments, giftings, competencies, experiences, and contexts that go into the manner in which a preacher delivers a message. You can see how communicators as different as Matt Chandler, H. B. Charles Jr., Tim Keller, John Piper, Eric Mason, Stephen Um, and Don Carson each bring unique styles to the service of the same concept—gospel-centered exposition. There may be as many styles as there are preachers—that is, if by *style* we simply mean *voice*.

If *style* refers to the manner in which any preacher delivers his sermon, I would say that there are three qualities that adorn the gospel in an excellent way:

▶ *Text-driven.* The sermon is driven by a biblical passage. It isn't just using Bible verses.

▶ *Appropriately passionate.* Preachers feel the biblical text in the same tone and tenor as the text itself and commensurate with their own personality and voice. The preacher should be sad when the Bible is sad and happy when the Bible is happy. Greater passion should be employed in delivering indicatives (what God has done) than in imperatives (what we are to do), so that congregations receive the impression over time that the "done" of the gospel is more glorious than the "do" of our obedience. It is possible to preach a gospel-centered sermon in content but, in reserving your passion for imperatives, inadvertently give the impression that the law matters more. As I've heard D. A. Carson say, "People don't get excited about what you tell them to be excited about; they get excited about what you're excited about."

▶ *Pastoral.* Sermons that seek to apply the truths of Scripture through the context of the gospel, not simply to practical matters but to matters of the heart and soul, find a greater magnitude in the impact of grace. Apply the gospel to doubt, to fear, to grief, to suffering, to confusion, to trauma. See how the gospel's application to heart-level needs will trump the law's application to felt needs. The latter is not unimportant, but the former will drive the latter in a way the reverse order never will.

What is most important in gospel-centered sermon preparation?

The most important thing is that you believe it. However long and deep your sermon prep will take you, make sure it is a devotional preparation as well as a homiletical preparation. Pray throughout and ask the Lord to help you embrace the truths you mean to preach. Channel your dedication to delight. The most important aspect of gospel-centered preaching is having a gospel-centered preacher.

I'm preaching the gospel, but my church isn't growing. Now what?

Be thoroughly introspective and ruthlessly honest about your faithfulness outside of the pulpit. Are you and your church faithfully sharing the gospel in evangelism? Are you making disciples? Are you applying the gospel organizationally? Is your church hospitable to outsiders, reaching out to those around them and remaining warm within for those who may respond to invitations? Does your church follow up with visitors? Are your regular attenders, all things considered, happy to be there?

Do whatever you can to ensure that your faithfulness in the gospel extends beyond preaching. You can't be perfect, and neither can your church. But be honest.

Now, if the answer to all those questions is an honest yes, consider that your steady pace is simply a season of preparation. Remember what Paul tells Timothy: "Preach the word; be ready in season and out of season" (2 Tim. 4:2). From this word we may infer that there are simply times where the Word of God is "out of season," perhaps even in a pastor's ministry. Paul's advice is not to embrace another message or strategy. He instructs Timothy to persevere: in season or out of season, keep preaching the gospel.

I am preaching gospel-centered sermons every week, but people are starting to complain that they are bored or tired of it.

Again, the need here is to be self-reflective and honest. Did they like your communication *prior* to the content transition? If so, it is possible either that you are still "working out the kinks" of gospel-centered preaching, or your congregation is. The solution is to work at it, improving in both your grasp of the application of the gospel, your ability to communicate it effectively, and even your communication style. Continue to pray that the Lord will soften the hearts of your people toward receptivity and enjoyment of the gospel, even as you pray that he will make you a better preacher. In the end, the only solution to "gospel fatigue" is more gospel. Whatever the problem is, it is never the gospel.

What is the place of church marketing or advertising in the gospel-centered paradigm?

There is nothing inherently wrong with letting the public know about the presence of your church and the opportunity to learn about God and the Bible there. The problem is not with the marketing per se but with the manner of marketing.

In our culture, people move frequently, and church advertising can be a good way to let Christians who have recently relocated know that you are an option. There may be Christians in your area who must leave their current church for a reason permitted by Scripture—the elders have disqualified themselves but are not removed, the gospel is not preached, orthodoxy is not affirmed, a family member has suffered abuse or trauma or has been otherwise victimized.

In addition, there is always the chance that legitimate spiritual seekers may be interested in learning more about Christianity and would discover your church as an option through these means. (I want to point out here, though, that the idea that there are a significant number of unbelievers interested in attending church just waiting for local churches to advertise their features is really overblown. These people may exist but not in significant numbers.)

When you advertise, here are some things to avoid:

▶ *Stating that your church is different than the others.* This is just a strange way to say you're better than the others. I know you are trying to communicate that your church may not be like the traditional or overbearing church experience of your potential visitor's upbringing, but the execution is just too problematic to be worth it. What it often sounds like is that your church has it figured out, and the others don't. Statements like these betray the unity of the church body in your community and position your church as in competition with others around you.

▶ *Describing service features in consumeristic terms.* There are appropriate adjectives for your music and preaching that apply to the content—"God-focused," "biblical." And there are adjectives that inadvertently demonstrate these features are for the worshiper. Avoid describing your worship elements like you're pitching a product. Even worse is promising giveaway items that visitors can win.

▶ *Listing features that make you sound desperate.* You can wear jeans lots of places. Most people know you can wear jeans at church now. Lots of places have coffee too. Nobody ever chose a church because it had coffee.

Preaching

How long should a gospel-centered sermon be?

There is no such thing as a gospel-centered sermon length. As with any kind of preaching, no bad sermon is short enough and no good sermon can really be too long.

Do justice to your text. Let the text dictate where you go. Do not test people's limits in patience and information absorption, but it's probably best to avoid little sermonettes and snapshot homilies. I think most congregations can weekly withstand good preaching that runs thirty to forty minutes. Most preachers shouldn't preach much longer than forty minutes, but if you think you're an exception, I suppose you might be.

Remember that nobody ever felt too forgiven or too liberated, so if you have to go longer, make sure that the message of grace is eating up most of that time.

What's wrong with video preaching?

I do not think there is anything inherently wrong with delivering preaching content by video. Meaning, no biblical text directly applies to this method. But I don't think it is wise for a few reasons.

First, it is not a good idea in our consumer age to un-incarnate anything. The virtual world of technology and social media have stunted the Western imagination and inhibited our ability to experience the fullness of relationships and vibrant community. It doesn't make sense to virtualize something so important to the life of a church as the Word of God preached. It implicitly communicates that presence isn't important. God did not send a DVD. He sent his Son, the Preacher.

Second, I am concerned about the message the video venue model sends about the church's identity and community. The primary reason one preacher is broadcast in multiple locations is because this preacher is seen as anointed or gifted beyond other local options. In other words, if a live preacher was used, the site would not be as viable as with the video preacher. I wonder how this logic does not immediately make the venue's viability suspect. Given the reality that many live preachers have congregations drawn to their abilities or personality, the video venue sets up the church's growth to become too intertwined with one person. If that person were to die or, worse, to fail morally, the complex can collapse.

Third, I have concerns about how the emphasis on video venues inhibits the growth of local campus pastors who are capable of preaching and for whom serving their congregations in the Word is a vital aspect of shepherding them. The less a preacher knows his audience, the more packaged and produced his preaching will be. Incarnated preaching is an extension of pastoral ministry commended by the Scriptures.

I have written much more on this subject in my book *The Prodigal Church*, and extensive thoughts can also be found in an episode of the *For the Church* podcast titled "Issues with Video Venues."[1] (See also the multisite question under the Discipleship and Community section.)

What is the place of altar calls and public invitations in a worship service?

Every gospel message ought to include some kind of invitation for response. "What must we do in response to this good news?" is a question you should anticipate as you prepare your message. But the place of public invitations is a bit tricky. Many have erred too far against the revivalistic pleading of evangelicalism past and declared them null and void forever.

And yet, I don't think we need rule out the altar call completely.

I don't think an altar call is necessary or normative in a church service, but if you do decide to incorporate some form of public invitation, here are some things to avoid:

> ▶ *Formulaic prayers to repeat.* This process often gives respondents false assurance. People may pray in reception of the gospel message and in repentance to receive Christ, but simply repeating words doesn't magically save anyone. I know most practitioners of this kind of public invitation don't think it does! But the inadvertent message is still there. You do not want to give any hint of personal assurance to people who merely repeat words.
> ▶ *Anonymity.* By making the congregation bow heads and close eyes while respondents may anonymously respond, you can give the impression that embracing Christianity is merely a personal decision that can be kept private. If a respondent cannot embrace Christ in a room full of Christians, what hope do we have of their witness in a world that hates God?
> ▶ *Undue pressure.* Whether through increasingly emotional pleadings or repetitive verses of an invitational song (or setting a contemplative mood with a modern worship song), avoid hints of manipulation or coercion.

An appropriate altar call may simply involve asking people who would like to respond to the gospel to come forward and receive counsel. You don't have to declare anything about their spiritual state in the moment or ask them to repeat a prayer. Have them come forward and be prepared to receive them with pastors or counselors who are trained to have gospel conversations.

Again, I don't think this practice ought to be normative for the worship gathering, but there is no reason it must be outlawed entirely if handled appropriately. You can, of course, simply remind those who'd like to respond that you are available and encourage them to seek you afterward. That is a fine way to issue an invitation as well.

Worship

Do multiple services work against the experience of gospel-centered community?

They don't have to. Multiple services, if conducted similarly and in a gospel-centered way, don't need to be any more antithetical to gospel application than small groups or even different sections of a sanctuary. Multiple services are not the ideal way to manage congregational growth, but they can work well if concentrated effort is made to keep services from representing multiple congregations in the same church.

How should we think about the atmosphere of the worship gathering or the creative elements employed in the service beyond the music?

Creative elements aside from music should be used sparingly and with adornment of the gospel in mind. A video that illustrates a gospel or biblical truth in a clear way is different from a movie clip, for instance. This doesn't mean a preacher may never use a movie clip, but this is not a normal way to conduct text-driven preaching of the gospel.

Excellence in all things is a worthy goal, but in the attractional paradigm too often excellence becomes an idol. Yet there is such a thing as being conspicuously mediocre! There is no virtue in being bland, boring, or otherwise blasé about the music, the preaching, or even the worship space.

Ask lots of questions about elements to be included. What do you lose to include certain features? Does this actually adorn the gospel or is it just something we think would be cool? How does it keep people undistracted from the Word? Will they be more tempted to walk away thinking "What a great set" or "What a great Savior"? Does this put the spotlight on us or on Jesus?

Ask a lot of why questions. Why are we doing this? Why do we think this is important? Why would this help people see Jesus more clearly?

Remember that every sanctuary has aesthetics. It's not about creating some puritan space devoid of character. It's not even about being uncreative. Wise pastors of the worship gathering work toward undistracting excellence. Wise pastors understand that very often, without intention, the medium becomes the message, so they are careful not to produce or perform what ought to be preached and pastored.

I would also caution against allowing creatives in your church to treat the worship service like a canvas upon which to freely express themselves. The church gathering is not about any particular kind of Christian expressing his or her feelings; it is about Christ. It is not there for anyone's art therapy or working out the restrictions of their upbringing. It's not about them (or you).

What factors should go into song choice for the worship gathering?

I do not envy worship leaders today. They are under tremendous amounts of pressure as congregations expect more of an experience in the music portion of a service. The desire for popular, exciting, and artistic songs that evoke certain worshipful feelings is always crouching at the church's door, seeking to devour. Those interested in pastoring through worship in song might want to consider these:

▶ *Biblical content.* Songs that draw directly from God's Word are to be preferred. If imagistic, does the image come from a Bible verse? Can you draw a direct line from lyrical content to biblical content? I don't believe this means you can only sing Bible passages—and this space is not a great place to discuss the varying perspectives on the regulative principle of worship—but songs that include biblical phrases and words in biblical contexts ought to be preferred over songs that may vaguely refer to something that might be in the Bible.

▶ *Gospel rehearsal.* Not every song needs to explicitly rehearse some facet of the atonement, the resurrection, or even Christ himself, but a gospel pattern should be evident. A good example of this would be singing a biblical psalm or a song based on a psalm. But while the entire singing time can include songs of lament, songs of grief, songs of need—all sourced in biblical content—the bulk of congregational singing ought to explicitly rehearse the gospel in some way. Songs about Jesus and his finished work or that retell the gospel narrative in some way ought to be prioritized.

▶ *Arrange for congregational singing.* This is where many attractional services drop the ball. Their content may be fine or mostly fine, but in presenting the music in a performance mode, they work against the congregation's ability to follow along. Or they create an atmosphere in which individuals experience personal worship times in the midst of others doing the same. Your songs should be straightforward enough for unskilled musicians to follow and sing along. What you sing should be on the screen or in a hymnal. The volume should be such that the congregation can hear themselves *and each other.* Hyper-focus on individual performers through lighting, musical solos, or other stage flourishes should be avoided. Lighting should be undistracting. The congregation shouldn't be in the dark. You may wonder what any of this has to do with gospel-centrality. I will tell you: because the gospel applied facilitates community, anything you do in a worship set must facilitate the experience of community as well. A worship gathering that feels like a production or performance is another way we communicate that the gospel is about your consumer desires and church is a product we're trying to sell you.

▶ *Contextualized style.* Contrary to popular opinion, style is not neutral. This does not mean that any particular genre of music is sinful. But it does mean that not every style of music is appropriate for use in a worship gathering. The limits are probably wider than many would anticipate, however. A worship song's style should take into consideration the content of the song, for instance. Are you singing an up-tempo song that is a lament? Are you singing a dirge-like song that has lyrics of joy? This usually happens as leaders try to evoke a mood based on the style rather than the content of the songs. Similarly, the worship style should be conducive to congregational singing. So fast-paced electronic, rock, or even bluegrass may be out. The worship style should not be distracting from the content but complementary to it. And finally, your style should be appropriate for your cultural context. In other words, trying to lead millennials in praise choruses from the '70s isn't a great idea, and neither is trying to lead an ethnically diverse congregation in Southern gospel.

Discipleship and Community

How should a pastor personally conduct discipleship relationships?

As mentioned in the relevant chapters, leading by example is a key point of applying the gospel organizationally. If you want to nurture a discipleship culture, you must be making disciples personally.

I think it is wise for every pastor to have at least two people he is discipling personally, perhaps more than that if he can meet with multiple disciples at once. It is advantageous also, for the disciple and for the disciple-maker, if at least one of these people is a new believer. I have found that discipling new believers helps keep pastors' spiritual lives fresh and vibrant, allowing them to remember what it's like to see the Scriptures and the gospel through new eyes.

Beyond that, it is good for pastors to disciple mostly more mature leaders, those not too far behind him, either mature lay leaders or those training for ministry.

Marshall and Payne's *The Trellis and the Vine* is an excellent resource for helping pastors think through their discipling relationships.

Should churches utilize the multisite method of facilitating church growth?

I think fewer should than do. I am not convinced multisite is an ideal method for facilitating growth, but there are churches that do it much better than others. If a church can share resources and a central elder board, but satellite campuses feature their own dedicated pastoral staff and live preaching, as well as an organic and contextual approach to mission in their location, I think they can be done well.

The best way to utilize the multisite approach, in my estimation, is to think of satellite campuses as proto—church plants and to launch them with this long-term strategy in mind. The way many churches execute multisite only exacerbates the problem of the attractional paradigm, feeding consumeristic mindsets of believers and unbelievers alike, but that doesn't mean they can never be done well or in ways that spread the gospel.

How should we think of student ministry in a gospel-centered church?

Student ministries centered on the gospel are tuned more closely to the life of the whole church. This means there is a concentration of biblical teaching, including expositional preaching. It also means that music is not much different from what is led in the church's corporate gathering. Additionally, the strongest student ministries make concerted efforts at discipleship and accountability and intergenerational relationships, as well as providing avenues for teenagers to serve the body at large in big and small ways.

The overarching points are to make sure student ministry does not shape a teenager consumer in such a way that "adult church" will be a shock to the system because it's so different, and in such a way as to provide as much interconnection between teenager and congregational body life as possible. Having a bubble isolating the student ministry serves neither student nor church.

This doesn't mean that fun and games should not be a part of student ministry life. They just shouldn't be the center of student ministry life. Most ministries, to embrace the gospel, end up having to choose between depth and width.

How should we think about children's ministry in a gospel-centered church?

The three primary instruments of teaching in a children's ministry environment are these:

▶ *Doctrinal catechesis.* Children's ministries should teach the basic tenets of Christian orthodoxy through rehearsal and memorization. Many times, this is done in a "question and answer" format that even small children take to right away. Catechesis, whether you use a formal catechism or not, is important because we are not currently raising theologically grounded Christians. Let's start young.

▶ *Whole Bible teaching.* Bible lessons should progress through the entire narrative of the Scriptures. Children's ministries ought to see if they can teach an overview of the entire Bible to children beginning in kindergarten and ending in fifth or sixth grade, with pauses for reviewing past material later. Of course, not every child will be present for each year, but the pattern of biblical rehearsal is formative and strengthening. It can be for teachers as well, as they get better at teaching similar books or passages every year. Perhaps a rotation every few years can help keep their studies fresh, if that is a concern.

▶ *Gospel over moralism.* The temptation, especially with biblical narratives, is to turn every Bible lesson into a moral lesson: be good, be nice, be sweet, act right. These are fine lessons and the Bible does teach them (and more) in its own way. But they do not and cannot change hearts like grace can. They do not and cannot place the treasure of Christ in a child's soul like the gospel can.

What would a meaningful membership process look like?

At a bare minimum, meaningful membership involves basic teaching of the Christian faith (perhaps using the church's statement of faith), the expectations and privileges of church membership, and any distinctives your church holds that may be unique or new to some prospective members. The point of the membership process is not merely to dispatch people to service roles, although that can be a component of the process. The membership process involves "ratifying" someone's professing of faith, making sure that those who formally covenant with your community, whether that involves voting rights or any other congregational access to decision-making, possess a credible witness and can contribute honestly to the doctrinal fidelity and evangelistic witness of your church.

You should also be making clear the obligations the church and the leaders have to individual members and families, such as the duty to provide care and counsel, nourishment, and discipline if necessary.

The process should include a class or series of classes that culminate with some kind of interview or meeting with a pastor or qualified leader.

How does church discipline work in a gospel-centered church?

If your church bylaws, membership covenant, or constitution do not provide an outline for what is entailed in church discipline, this is something to discuss with your pastoral team. In many churches, discipline is arbitrary, punitive, and unpastoral, which is why so many churches don't practice it at all.

Biblical church discipline always has the restoration of the repentant as its aim. In some cases, leaders may need to protect a member from the church. In others, they may need to protect the church from a member. Discipline helps us navigate the differences, discerning repentance, mercy, and appropriate boundaries or principles for reconciliation.

The principles and order laid out in Matthew 18, Titus 3:10–11, and 1 Corinthians 5 ought to be followed with great care, courageous conviction, and gracious concern for all involved.

How do we phase out old programs that don't fit our transition plans?

Eliminating stale programs or ministry departments that no longer fit the vision for the church can be made even more difficult if the program has existed for a long time and especially if there is a leader or advocate still devotedly attached.

First, ask if it's really necessary to cut it or if you're just in "cut everything" mode. Does what you stand to win outweigh what you stand to lose?

If so, do not cut the program without engaging in conversation with the leader or leaders involved. Overcommunicate. Explain. Ask them to help you brainstorm alternatives that they can be a part of.

Can you repurpose the program instead of cutting it? Can it be used for mission?

If a building or a building space is involved, can you repurpose it for gospel mission? Use it to exercise hospitality or acts of service to the community?

In the end, you must do what is best for the whole church and for gospel mission. Try to win the leader to these concerns and minimize talk about popularity, budgetary concerns, and the like.

Mission

Should a gospel-centered church employ the missional practice of "belonging before believing"?

Yes, so long as we clearly define what "belonging" means. An unbeliever should not be a member, serve in another area, or be in a leadership position for which a credible profession of faith is integral.

However, our church should be a hospitable place and a gracious place in which those genuinely seeking answers to their spiritual questions can hear the gospel with patience, tenderness, and joy. Community groups can host unbelievers interested in observing Christian community in action. The weekend worship gathering should be a welcoming place for any kind of visitor, including those who do not know Jesus.

Participating in the church at these lower levels of community relationships can be profound, formative, and compelling to those who will believe the gospel.

What does missions look like in a gospel-centered church?

Many churches support missions projects of all kinds, but it is common to see churches lending financial, material, or other kinds of support for missions with obscure gospel connection or vague doctrinal beliefs. Social justice efforts, rightly understood, are all very fine, but gospel mission requires gospel content. Otherwise, we simply preach the good news of our works.

Therefore, whether in support of local or foreign missionaries or local or global service causes, gospel-centered churches seek to support gospel-centered people and organizations.

It is also important to keep this support visible and verbal so that your church can be shaped over time to value God's continuing mission in the earth themselves.

What is the place of outreach events or revival ministries in the church today?

In our day, these means are increasingly cultural obstacles to authentic gospel witness. It doesn't mean they should never be conducted or that nobody ever hears the gospel and is saved at them, but these kinds of evangelistic strategies serve more in these days to please traditional Christians than to redeem secular unbelievers.

The best witness event is your church gathering, though it is aimed primarily at believers. The best evangelistic strategy is your well-equipped church members sent out from this gathering to be on mission in the world the other six days of the week.

Leadership and Ministry

What should a timeline for change look like?

Church and community contexts are too varied to offer a schedule for change. My biggest lament in writing this book is that it could not be *that* practical. I cannot offer a formula for change, mainly because the gospel so often subverts our formulas. This is a book against pragmatism, remember?

Creating a timeline may be impractical because of the variety of situations represented by readers. However, there are some general concerns that could be worked through to determine an appropriate timeline for your context:

▶ *Top Tier Issues (Immediate Change)*—Chief among these would be the unifying of directional leadership on the vision and then the change in preaching. Preaching is perhaps the first and best thing you can control and immediately change without causing too much distress in your congregation, at least at the first point of change. Also included in this tier could be music content and the worship gathering in general. That is the primary point of congregational direction, so it makes sense to work through that transition first.

▶ *Second Tier Issues (Necessary Change)*—This tier could include a church feature like worship music if you anticipate that change should be less abrupt, and it includes institutional health like making sure pastors/elders are qualified, meaningful membership is established, and the budget reflects values of gospel and mission.

▶ That these issues are necessary does not mean the change should be immediate. Discern your context and its most pressing needs. Discern your congregation's threshold for change. Perhaps take one issue at a time. Move slowly through it, overcommunicating, showing your cards, and patiently showing from the Bible the importance for the change. Take as long as is necessary while maintaining obedient progress. When you're finished, give the congregation time to rest before beginning the next process.

At my last pastorate, we needed to both clean up the membership rolls and embrace plurality of eldership. Rather than do this simultaneously, I opted to do the former first. It took a year. Then I decided to tackle eldership. This was a new concept to the church and had the potential of being divisive. It took three years from start to finish— one year to teach our existing leaders and get them on board, one year to gradually teach the congregation through a variety of means, at the end of which the church voted to change their bylaws to allow for elders, and finally one year to assess candidates and establish four additional elders.

▶ *Third Tier Issues (Important but Gradual Changes)*—These changes are not unnecessary, but they often are fraught with more difficulty. You may want to start addressing them on the leadership level right away, but implementation of actual changes may need to come later and more gradually. This tier likely includes long-standing programs, discipleship processes that are no longer fruitful (some Sunday School formats, some gender- or age-specific ministries, etc.), and student or children's ministry. Children's ministry is typically easier to change, as most parents are not overly invested in the curriculum their children are receiving.

▶ It is when the children are old enough to begin expressing boredom or disapproval with youth events that parents become inordinately concerned with how entertaining student ministry ought to be. Because of this, change should happen incrementally, conscientiously, and patiently. Student ministers should have the backing of the pastoral staff or elders, so they are not left to fend for themselves against angry parents.

What should a gospel-centered budget look like?

Priorities should include personnel—because those who labor in preaching and teaching and other vocational service of the gospel are worthy of the honor—and missions. Remember that anybody's budget tells us what they treasure, and this includes churches.

How do I handle angry church members?

Consulting the chapter on gracious leading of change, do your best to listen well, not take things personally, be transparent, and encourage them along. Many people who are angry about change are simply confused or discomforted. It is rarely a philosophical or theological concern driving the irritation. If it is, do your best to address the issue using the Bible to show the strength of gospel-centrality.

If they cannot be persuaded to seek peace with the transition and joyfully cooperate, remind them biblically of their obligations to seek to be at peace, to serve the church with cheer, and not to give their leaders cause for groaning. If that fails, it may be time to suggest they transition membership to another church more aligned with their preferences. This is a regrettable and lamentable circumstance, but it is frequently necessary for members who cannot, for whatever reason, agree with the importance of the gospel-centered vision.

If they don't think leaving is the right thing to do and decide to stay—peaceably without causing division—pray for them, encourage them, and hope they see the value of the vision as they participate in worship and witness the vision take shape.

If they do not leave and persist in anger, especially to the point of sinful division, gossip, or subversion of the mission, it is likely time to bring up the prospect of formal discipline. Follow the biblical pattern and biblical warnings. Paul says what to do with a divisive person (Titus 3:10).

How do I shepherd uncooperative staff members?

The conviction necessary to lead a church transition graciously is something that ought to be shared. This was Pastor Josh's concern about his old friend Pastor Bob. He knew Bob wasn't antagonistic. But he also knew that Bob's ambivalence or apathy would not serve the transition in the long run. So Josh began to pray about and process the possibility of having to ask Bob to step down.

This process is never fun. It is, for many pastors, the worst part of leading a growing or changing church. Even some loyal staff members cannot be brought along because they lack the necessary aptitude or attitude to effectively partner in the leadership of the transition.

First, bend over backward to help. Do not hold up the prospect of being fired as motivation. Cheerlead and encourage. Supply with resources. Take them to conferences. Ask them questions that help them process the gospel and its application in their own ways. They may come around yet.

Don't expect them to quickly be where you are now when they are simply where you were recently yourself. How were you helped to understand? Help that way.

If over time you discern an inability to effectively collaborate in key ways that help the church, it may be time to have a heart to heart conversation. Make sure they know you're not mad, they're not in trouble, there's no sin issue involved, and you're not asking them to leave the church if they'd like to stay. Gently and tenderly, with regrets and restraint, advise them that you don't believe they're the best fit for the current trajectory.

Offer to help them in any way you can, including supplying recommendations or references if they decide to move to another position elsewhere. Provide a generous severance package. Do not permit gossip. Shepherd the exit well by staying tuned in to the staffer and their family. Absorb any hits you need to absorb to help them process any hurt.

Pray.

How can we help older members make the transition successfully?

It is not extremely common for attractional churches to have many older members reluctant to change. This situation is more common in traditional-to-gospel-centered transitions. Nevertheless, it is a frequent enough concern to address here.

Remember that so much is changing for older folks. The world is increasingly uncomfortable and unrelatable. When we change what they know at church, we add one more level of discomfort and unrelatability to their world, and we do it in the one place that many have always felt some measure of belonging and participation. So be empathetic about how much more disruptive it is for the older generation to change than it is for the younger.

Paul says, "Do no rebuke an older man but encourage him as you would a father" (1 Tim. 5:1). Do whatever you can to entreat older members to help. Ask for prayer, ask for advice, ask for volunteers in discipleship processes and mentoring. This is one of the greatest stated needs from the younger generation and one of the greatest reluctances on the part of the older generation. Do what you can to eradicate those generational barriers. Remind them gently that there is no retirement from the Christian life and then encourage them to embrace places of influence. Explain patiently. Stay present. Stay humble.

Recommended Resources

The Gospel and Gospel-Centrality

Matt Chandler, *The Explicit Gospel*

Ray Ortlund, *The Gospel: How the Church Portrays the Beauty of Christ*

Milton Vincent, *A Gospel Primer for Christians*

Jared C. Wilson, *Gospel Wakefulness*

Church Culture and Philosophy

Thomas E. Bergler, *The Juvenilization of American Christianity*

J. R. Briggs and Bob Hyatt, *Ministry Mantras*

Tim Chester and Steve Timmis, *Total Church: A Radical Reshaping around Gospel and Community*

Mark Dever, *Nine Marks of a Healthy Church*

Ajith Fernando, *Jesus-Driven Ministry*

Michael Horton, *Christless Christianity: The Alternative Gospel of the American Church*

Skye Jethani, *The Divine Commodity*

Tim Keller, *Center Church*

Jonathan Leeman, *Word-Centered Church*

Pastoral Ministry

H. B. Charles Jr., *On Pastoring*

Zack Eswine, *The Imperfect Pastor*

John Piper, *Brothers, We Are Not Professionals*

Bob Thune, *Gospel-Centered Eldership*
Jared C. Wilson, *The Pastor's Justification*
Timothy Witmer, *The Shepherd Leader*

Preaching and Teaching

Bryan Chapell, *Christ-Centered Preaching*
Zack Eswine, *Preaching to a Post-Everything World*
Tim Keller, *Preaching: Communicating Faith in an Age of Skepticism*
Jonathan Leeman, *Reverberation: How God's Word Brings Light,*
    Freedom, and Action to His People
Tony Merida, *The Christ-Centered Expositor: A Field Guide for Word-*
    Driven Disciple Makers
Trevin Wax, *Gospel-Centered Teaching*

Leadership and Discipleship

Mike Ayers, *Power to Lead*
Jonathan Dodson, *Gospel-Centered Discipleship*
Eric Geiger and Kevin Peck, *Designed to Lead*
Colin Marshall and Tony Payne, *The Trellis and the Vine: The Ministry*
    Mind-Shift That Changes Everything
Thom Rainer, *Who Moved My Pulpit?: Leading Change in the Church*
Scott Sauls, *From Weakness to Strength*
Brandon Smith, ed., *Make, Mature, Multiply*
Scott Thomas, *Gospel Coach: Shepherding Leaders to Glorify God*
Paul Tripp, *Instruments in the Redeemer's Hands: People in Need of*
    Change Helping People in Need of Change

Worship

Bryan Chapell, *Christ-Centered Worship: Letting the Gospel Shape*
    Our Practice
Mike Cosper, *Rhythms of Grace*
Bob Kauflin, *Worship Matters*
Stephen Miller, *Worship Leaders, We Are Not Rock Stars*
Jared C. Wilson, *Gospel Shaped Worship*

Community

Dietrich Bonhoeffer, *Life Together*
Tim Chester and Steve Timmis, *Everyday Church*
Jeff Vanderstelt, *Saturate*

Student and Children's Ministry

Cameron Cole (ed.), *Gospel-Centered Youth Ministry*
Brian Dembowczyk, *Gospel-Centered Kids Ministry*
Elyse Fitzpatrick and Jessica Thompson, *Give Them Grace*
Jack Klumpenhower, *Show Them Jesus: Teaching the Gospel to Kids*
Sally Lloyd-Jones, *The Jesus Storybook Bible*
Bob Thune and Will Walker, *The Gospel-Centered Life for Teens*

Websites

The Gospel Coalition, thegospelcoalition.org
For the Church, ftc.co
9 Marks Ministries, 9marks.org
Gospel-Centered Discipleship, gcdiscipleship.com

Podcasts

Pastors' Talk with Jonathan Leeman and Mark Dever
For the Church with Jared C. Wilson
The Village Church

Acknowledgments

This project is the culmination of twenty-five years of ministry in, service to, and heart for the church. I am deeply indebted to more precious saints (and more than a few seekers) than I can count. To attempt to name them all proves too daunting. But I would be remiss if I did not mention a few mentors, colleagues, and friends who have especially helped me along the way, namely—

Clint Pressley, Steve Benninger, Chris Lewis, Dave Leandre, Matt and Mitch Bedzyk, Steven Leatherbury, Brandon Freeman, and Jeff Dodge, all awesome pastors who have given me windows into their ministries and have allowed me to learn from them in big ways and serve with them in small ways;

Ray Ortlund, to whom I am incredibly indebted and hopelessly devoted;

Matt Chandler, Mark Dever, and Tim Keller, whose ministries have blessed and shaped me in ways incalculable;

Nathan Rose, Sam Bierig, and David Bronson, my pastors at Liberty Baptist Church, who shepherd us with such grace;

the young bucks of the Pastoral Training Center at Liberty Baptist, who enthusiastically suit up and show up, and have given a tired guy a second lease on ministry life;

the dear brothers in my 2018 ministry coaching cohort, who have helped me think through more carefully the application of gospel-centrality in churches of various sizes, temperaments, and contexts all over the country;

Don Gates, the best darn agent a writer could ask for;

my editor Ryan Pazdur and the stellar team at Zondervan, who believed in me and, more importantly, in the project;

all the churches and organizations that let me workshop most of this material in conferences and consulting sessions over the last three years;

and most importantly, Becky, Macy, and Grace, whose generosity with me to the ministry of itinerant preaching and incessant writing will be fully rewarded, I am sure, in the age to come.

I love you all.

Notes

Foreword

1. Charles Spurgeon, *Lectures to My Students* (repr., Grand Rapids: Zondervan, 1954), 343.

Chapter 1: The Dilemma

1. For a longer and more detailed evaluation of the motives and methods of the attractional church, see my book *The Prodigal Church: A Gentle Manifesto Against the Status Quo* (Wheaton, IL: Crossway, 2015) alongside or shortly after reading this book. You don't have to have read that book to read this one, but it will certainly flesh out more concerns—both biblical and logical—about the attractional paradigm than I am able to explore here.
2. Greg L. Hawkins and Cally Parkinson, *REVEAL: Where Are You?* (South Barrington, IL: Willow Creek Association, 2007). See also "Willow Creek Repents?," *Christianity Today* (online), October 2007, http://www.christianitytoday.com/pastors/2007/october-online-only/willow-creek-repents.html.
3. Note the research included in Ed Stetzer, Richie Stanley, and Jason Hayes, *Lost and Found: The Younger Unchurched and the Churches That Reach Them* (Nashville: B&H, 2009), in particular the findings that as it pertains to church programming, the younger generation highlighted a desire for "authentic encounters," "relational equity," and relationships over church programs (71). See also James Emery White, *Meet Generation Z: Understanding and Reaching the New Post-Christian World* (Grand Rapids: Baker, 2017).
4. Lydia Saad, "Sermon Content Is What Appeals to Most Churchgoers," Gallup, 14 April 2017, https://news.gallup.com/poll/208529/sermon-content-appeals-churchgoers.aspx.

5. Kate Shellnutt, "The Hottest Thing at Church Is Not Your Pastor or Worship Leader," *Christianity Today*, 18 April 2017, https://www.christianitytoday.com/news/2017/april/gallup-hottest-thing-at-church-not-pastor-worship.html.

6. Ed Stetzer, "Seeker Comprehensible Preaching . . . Without Dumbing Down," *The Exchange* (blog), *Christianity Today*, 8 June 2016, https://www.christianitytoday.com/edstetzer/2016/june/preaching-without-dumbing-down.html.

7. "The Bible in America: 6-Year Trends," Barna, 15 June 2016, https://www.barna.com/research/the-bible-in-america-6-year-trends/.

8. "Reasons 18-to-22 Year Olds Drop Out of Church," Lifeway Research, 7 August 2007, https://lifewayresearch.com/2007/08/07/reasons-18-to-22-year-olds-drop-out-of-church/. See also Sally Morgenthaler, "Worship as Evangelism," *Rev! Magazine* (May/June 2007): 49–50, http://nancybeach.typepad.com/nancy_beach/files/morgenthaler_article.pdf.

9. See Scott Thumma and Warren Bird, "Not Who You Think They Are: A Profile of the People Who Attend America's Megachurches," Hartford Institute for Religion Research online, Leadership Network and Hartford Seminary, 2009, http://hirr.hartsem.edu/megachurch/megachurch_attender_report.htm. This study revealed that most attenders of megachurches are not unchurched yet have been in their current church less than five years.

10. "What REVEAL Reveals," *Christianity Today*, 27 February 2008, https://www.christianitytoday.com/ct/2008/march/11.27.html.

11. Note the highest yet reporting of respondents identifying as "nones" in the religious survey from the Pew Research Center: "Faith in Flux," Pew Forum, February 2011, http://www.pewforum.org/2009/04/27/faith-in-flux/.

12. See the religious, ethnic, and economic analysis of the aforementioned Pew Forum research as shown in Luis Lugo, "The Decline of Institutional Religion," Faith Angle Forum, 18 March 2013, https://www.washingtonpost.com/r/2010-2019/WashingtonPost/2013/03/25/Editorial-Opinion/Graphics/Pew-Decline-of-Institutional-Religion.pdf.

13. Sally Morgenthaler, "Worship as Evangelism," *Rev! Magazine* (May/June 2007): 49, http://nancybeach.typepad.com/nancy_beach/files/morgenthaler_article.pdf.

14. Scott Thumma and Warren Bird, "Not Who You Think They Are."

Chapter 2: The Metrics That Don't Tell Us Everything

1. Kelly Shattuck, "7 Startling Facts: An Up-Close Look at Church Attendance in America," Church Leaders, 10 April 2018, https://churchleaders.com/pastors/pastor-articles/139575-7-startling-facts-an-up-close-look-at-church-attendance-in-america.html.

2. Charles Spurgeon, *The Soul Winner* (Grand Rapids: Eerdmans, 1963), 19.

3. J. R. Briggs and Bob Hyatt, *Ministry Mantras: Language for Cultivating Kingdom Culture* (Downers Grove, IL: Intervarsity Press, 2016), 132.

4. David Hertweck, *Good Kids, Big Events, and Matching T-Shirts: Changing the Conversation on Health in Youth Ministry* (Springfield, MO: My Healthy Church, 2015), 83–84.

5. Jonathan Edwards, *Distinguishing Marks of a Work of the Spirit of God*, in *Jonathan Edwards on Revival* (Carlisle, PA: Banner of Truth, 1965), 97.

6. Edwards, *Distinguishing Marks*, 91.

7. Spurgeon, *The Soul Winner*, 19.

Chapter 3: The Five Metrics That Matter Most

1. Jonathan Edwards, *Distinguishing Marks of a Work of the Spirit of God*, in *Jonathan Edwards on Revival* (Carlisle, PA: Banner of Truth, 1965), 110.

2. Edwards, *Distinguishing Marks*, 110.

3. Edwards, *Distinguishing Marks*, 111.

4. Edwards, *Distinguishing Marks*, 113.

5. Russell Moore and Andy Stanley, "Leadership, Preaching, and Cultural Engagement," video, ERLC Conference, 25 August 2016, https://erlc.com/resource-library/event-messages/leadership-preaching-and-cultural-engagement.

6. Andy Stanley with Thomas Horrocks, "Why 'The Bible Says So' Is Not Enough Anymore," *Outreach*, 9 November 2016, http://www.outreachmagazine.com/features/19900-the-bible-says-so.html

7. David Prince on Twitter (September 30, 2016), https://twitter.com/davideprince/status/781963836177907712.

8. Stanley with Horrocks, "Why 'The Bible Says So' Is Not Enough Anymore."

9. Stanley with Horrocks, "Why 'The Bible Says So' Is Not Enough Anymore."

10. Stanley with Horrocks, "Why 'The Bible Says So' Is Not Enough Anymore."

11. Edwards, *Distinguishing Marks*, 115.

12. A version of what follows originally appeared in Jared C. Wilson, "Why Theological Study Is for Everyone," *Tabletalk Magazine*, 1 April 2014, https://www.ligonier.org/learn/articles/why-theological-study-everyone/.

13. Edwards, *Distinguishing Marks*, 116.

14. Mark Dever, "Biblical Church Growth: 1 Thessalonians 3:12–4:12," 9Marks, from the Toledo Reformed Theological Conference, 27 April 2002, https://www.9marks.org/article/biblical-church-growth-i-thessalonians-312-412/.

Chapter 4: Putting the Gospel in the Driver's Seat

1. B. B. Warfield, "The Biblical Idea of Revelation," *The Works of Benjamin B. Warfield*, vol. 1, *Revelation and Inspiration* (Baker: Grand Rapids, 2000), 3.

2. Maurice Roberts, "The Prayer for Revival (Psalm 89)," oChristian.com, http://articles.ochristian.com/article2562.shtml.

3. Nancy Scammacca Lewis, "Lessons Learned from the REVEAL Spiritual Life Study," in *Bible in Mission*, Regnum Edinburgh Centenary Series 18, ed. Pauline Hoggarth, Fergus MacDonald, Bill Mitchell, and Knud Jørgensen (Eugene, OR: Wipf and Stock, 2014), 257.

4. "Engaging Scripture Is the #1 Predictor of Spiritual Health and Growth," American Bible Society, https://www.americanbible.org/uploads/content/engaging-scripture-is-the-1-predictor-of-spiritual-health-and-growth.pdf.

5. Joel Lindsey, "What Is a Gospel-Centered, Missional Church, and Why Do We Need One?" *For the Church*, 28 April 2015, https://ftc.co/resource-library/blog-entries/why-we-need-a-gospel-centered-missional-church.

6. Timothy Keller, *Center Church: Doing Balanced Ministry in Your City* (Grand Rapids: Zondervan, 2012), 36.

Chapter 5: Steering from the Stage

1. For more on the gospel's forming of the worship gathering, see my *Gospel Shaped Worship* Bible study curriculum (The Good Book Company and The Gospel Coalition, 2015).

2. Martyn Lloyd-Jones, *The Puritans: Their Origins and Successors* (Edinburgh: Banner of Truth, 1987), 360.

3. This is a slight restating of the definition of preaching I argue for in my book *The Pastor's Justification* (Wheaton, IL: Crossway, 2013). A fuller treatment can be found there.

4. Charles Spurgeon, "Christ Precious to Believers" in *Sermons of Rev. C. H. Spurgeon of London* (London: Robert Carter and Brothers, 1883), 356–57.

5. Ray Ortlund, "Taking Notes in Church?," *Christ Is Deeper Still* (blog), 31 May 2011, https://www.thegospelcoalition.org/blogs/ray-ortlund/taking-notes-in-church/.

Chapter 6: Building Your Service around Beholding

1. N. T. Wright, *For All God's Worth: True Worship and the Calling of the Church* (Grand Rapids: Eerdmans, 1997), 74.

2. Skye Jethani, *The Divine Commodity: Discovering a Faith Beyond Consumer Christianity* (Grand Rapids: Zondervan, 2009), 72–73.

3. Bob Kauflin, *Worship Matters: Leading Others to Encounter the Greatness of God* (Wheaton, IL: Crossway, 2008), 99.

4. Wright, *For All God's Worth*, 10.

5. Matt Capps, "The Beauty of Congregational Worship," *For the Church*, 10 November 2015, https://ftc.co/resource-library/blog-entries/the-beauty-of-congregational-worship.